My Favorite Intermissions

My Favorite Intermissions

by VICTOR BORGE

and ROBERT SHERMAN

Drawings by Thomas Winding

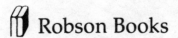 Robson Books

FIRST PUBLISHED IN GREAT BRITAIN IN 1982
BY ROBSON BOOKS LTD., BOLSOVER HOUSE,
5–6 CLIPSTONE STREET, LONDON W1P 7EB.
COPYRIGHT © 1971 VICTOR BORGE

British Library Cataloguing in Publication Data

Borge, Victor
  My favourite intermissions.
  1. Music—Anecdotes, facetiae, satire, etc.
  I. Title   II. Sherman, Robert
  780'.207   ML65

  ISBN 0-86051-204-5

Designed by Miller/Schleifer

Printed in Great Britain by
Biddles Ltd, Guildford, Surrey

Table of Contents

OVERTURE

"Every theatre is a lunatic asylum," said a friend of Franz Liszt, "but opera is the ward for incurables." I don't know what Liszt answered, but he left his nine operas unfinished, and lived to a sane old age.

The subject of opera as it is presented here should qualify as a documentary of fascinating and surprising behavior of some of history's Greats and the often ridiculous and hilarious occurrences in which they were involved, deliberately or by fate or accident.

And you don't have to know one tone from another to be able to enjoy it.

Bob Sherman[1] and I feel well qualified to write about operas. We have both — together and individually — slept through some of the best ones.

When you have finished reading the book, you'll hardly need any further proof that truth is stranger than fiction. Perhaps you will agree with me that it's also funnier.

Should you, however, be inclined to question the reliability of what you're being told . . . don't!

[1]Between chapters, Robert Sherman is Program Director of WQXR and a music critic for the New York Times.

All is based on facts as you will find if you look it up. But you don't have to because we already did.

If you have never attended an opera and the following chapters should create in you a desire to do so, please stay long enough to enjoy an intermission! It's often the best part of the evening.

V.B.

Curtain Up

My Favorite Intermissions

Johann Sebastian Bach

Johann Sebastian Bach is the first of the Three B's. As a matter of fact, he came so first that in his day he was just about the only B around.[1] Of course, there were dozens of other musical Bachs, and even some Baachs, but they were just relatives. I suppose you're wondering why I'm starting a book on opera with a chapter about a composer who never wrote any. For one thing, I don't care for books that tell you what you already know! Besides, Johann Sebastian wrote oratorios that are just as long as operas, and some of his cantatas are just as dull as some operas, and I'm sure that he would have been delighted to compose miles and miles of operas if anybody had ever bothered asking him to. I have a theory, incidentally, which might answer the question of why Bach didn't write operas. But I'm saving it for later, where it won't do so much harm.

Chips Off the Old Bach

The first musical Bach was named Vitus, or Veit for short. Some people called him "simple old Veit," but usually not when he could hear them. He used to sit around outside his windmill, playing his lute in time to the grinding noises. Sometimes the wind died down, and then Veit went inside

[1] Unless you count Buxtehude, and nobody counts Buxtehude much any more.

and had children. Two of his grandsons were named Johannes and Christoph, and (pay attention now) Johannes' second wife, Hedwig Lämmerhirt, had a brother named Valentin Lämmerhirt, and Valentin's daughter, Elizabeth, married Johann Ambrosius, who was Christoph's son by his first wife, Maria Magdalena Gräbler. The annoying thing was that Johann Ambrosius Bach was half of a pair of twins, and he and his brother looked so much alike that even their wives had trouble telling them apart. They tried writing music, but that wasn't much help since their styles were so similar that their wives couldn't tell their compositions apart either. Eventually, Ambrosius had a bright idea, and about nine months later, on March 21st, 1685, along came Johann Sebastian Bach. At last, Ambrosius' wife could identify her husband. He was the one the baby called Papa.

Home-town News

Johann Sebastian Bach was born in Eisenach, and though you wouldn't have thought so to look at the place, it was already a fairly famous town. It had two rivers, a forest, some salt springs, and the Wartburg Castle, where minstrels used to hang out as long ago as the 12th century. Saint Elizabeth of Hungary lived in the Wartburg when she was on tour, and in 1207 they held a minnesong contest there which Wagner later converted into a maxi-opera.[2] In 1521, Martin Luther moved into the Wartburg and sang hymns. The contest was over already, but Luther didn't seem to notice. A few of the local citizens warned him about the food, but he paid no attention to that either. He'd just finished with the Diet of Worms, and figured a little Wartburger wasn't going to hurt him.

[2]See Tannhäuser.[3]

[3]Better yet, hear Tannhäuser.

Early Days

Naturally, Johann Sebastian became a musician like the rest of the Bach family. He learned to sing, and he played the harpsichord and the organ and the violin, and soon he began studying the works of all the old masters he could find. He studied Jeep and Kerll and Bohm and Fux, and he studied Schop and Schutz and Scheidt and Schein[4] and then he started to compose, himself. He figured that *somebody* had better write some decent music. Bach's first job was as organist and choirmaster in the town of Arnstadt, and everything would have been great except that he was forever in trouble with the authorities. They hauled Bach up on charges of insulting one of his students. (Bach had called him a "Zippelfagottist." Then again, the student called Bach a "Hundsfott," which wasn't so nice either.[5]) And they complained that he went to a neighboring town to inspect a new organ and didn't show up again for four months. They were furious at Bach for making his organ introductions so long, and they were even more furious at him for making the hymns so short. They badgered him for making the harmonies so strange that they could hardly tell which hymn they were sleeping through. To top it off, a resolution was unanimously passed in the Council "thereupon to ask Bach by what right he recently caused a strange maiden to be invited into the choir loft, and let her make music there."[6]

Promotion

Bach's next job was as the town organist in Mulhausen,

[4]Not to mention Herpol, Hermann, Heermann and Hammerschmidt.

[5]A Zippelfagottist is a bassoon player who makes noises like a nanny goat. In this case, possibly vice versa.

[6]That was no strange maiden, Bach said, that was his cousin . . .

and as soon as he signed a contract agreeing to "avoid all unseemly society and suspicious company," he moved in, bag, baggage and cousin. The salary was about the same—a little under fifty dollars a year—but at least the fringe benefits were better. Bach was promised three pounds of fish, two cords of wood and fifty-four bushels of corn, plus home delivery of several dozen fagots.[7]

Family Life

Obviously Bach couldn't eat all that corn by himself, so he moved in with Maria Barbara Bach. That was no cousin, he said, that was his wife, and to prove it, he had seven children with her. Later, he married again and had thirteen more children.[8] Finally all the corn was gone, so Bach stopped having children and moved to Leipzig, where he became the Music Master at St. Thomas' School. The pay was even better here, but Bach had to sign another contract agreeing to stay sober, and not to let his students sing at funerals without cutting in the Burgomeister on the profits. He also had to promise not to make his cantatas too long. Bach got around that last part easily, of course. He just made his oratorios too long instead.[9]

Fun and Games

Although Bach often specialized in sacred pieces, he liked to have a good time as well as the next fellow. I've already mentioned his twenty children.[10] Well, he also wrote a number of cantatas that are as bright and cheerful as any comic opera

[7]Fagots were bundles of sticks used for kindling, in case you were worried there for a minute.

[8]Possibly fourteen.

[9]He composed some short pieces too, including the Air on the G String. You can't get much shorter than that.

[10]Possibly twenty-one.

[15]

of the period. One of the brightest and most cheerful of them was prepared for the birthday party of Duke Christian of Saxe-Weissenfels. Duke Christian didn't fool around when it came to birthdays. Especially his. He invited a couple of hundred friends over, and for three weeks they had fox hunts in Weissenfels during the day, and Saxe parties in the palace at night. Bach's Cantata came in between, and was mainly about how Sheep could Safely Graze because the Duke's friends had chased away all the foxes.

Other Activities

Bach also wrote lighthearted music for college graduations, civic installations, local appearances by visiting dignitaries, and wedding parties. He liked birthday cantatas best, because he could sell the same piece over and over again just by changing the name of the customer. Speaking of customers, Bach had some pretty fancy ones. When he composed a Serenade for Augustus II,[11] the King was so pleased that he ordered the poem printed on white satin, bound in deep scarlet velvet, with gilt tassels and gold fringes, and brought to him in a torchlight procession on a silver platter. The words, that is. Bach's music he misplaced. Bach also wrote a Cantata for the engagement party of Princess Amalia, dedicating it to her father, His Most Serene Highness, the Mighty Prince and Lord, Frederick Augustus, King in Poland, Grand Duke in Lithuania, Reuss, Prussia, Mazovia, Samogitia, Kyovia, Vollhynia, Podolia, Podlachia, Liefland, Smolensk, Severia and Czernicovia, Duke of Saxony, Julich, Cleve, Berg, Engern and Westphalia, Archmarshal and Elector of the Holy Roman Empire, Landgrave in Thuringia, Margrave of Meissen, also

---

[11]Augustus had three hundred and sixty-five illegitimate children by the time he was through.[12]

[12]No wonder he was through!

Upper and Lower Lausitz, Burgrave of Magdeburg, Prince and Count of Henneberg, Count of the Marck, Ravensberg and Barby, Lord of Ravenstein, and My Most Gracious King, Elector and Master. You could look it up, because the King kept it proudly ever after. The dedication, that is. Bach's music he misplaced.

With Cream and Sugar

The closest Bach ever came to writing a real opera was in his Cantata #211. It has a plot, it has recitatives and arias, and it's simply called The Coffee Cantata. If money had been appropriated for costumes and scenery, it could easily have been an opera.[13] Bach became quite an expert on coffee, by the way, and for years conducted weekly concerts at Zimmermann's Coffee House in Leipzig.[14]

Coffee Break

The reason Bach picked coffee for his Cantata is that coffee drinking used to be considered a wicked vice. All sorts of laws were passed against it, and some places even had spies roaming the city, sniffing the air and trying to catch people in the act of roasting coffee beans. "It is disgusting to notice the increase in the quantity of coffee used by my subjects," read one edict from Frederick the Great, "and this must be prevented. His Majesty was brought up on beer, and so were his Ancestors and his Officers. Many battles have been fought and won by soldiers nourished on beer, and the King does not believe that coffee-drinking soldiers can be depended upon to

[13]Bach never spent money needlessly. Once he wrote a whole sonata for flute and harpsichord just because he had three empty staves of music paper left over at the bottom of a double concerto.

[14]From 8 to 10 P.M., Fridays. (adv.)

endure hardships or to beat his enemies in case of war."[15] Women were also told that drinking coffee would make them sterile.[16]

[15]I'm sure the fact that Frederick owned part interest in a brewery had nothing to do with his feelings on the subject.

[16]His wives loved coffee, so Bach knew better.

Mainline Music

As for the Coffee Cantata itself, it's the original generation gap story. "Don't we have a hundred thousand troubles with our children," moans the father in his very first aria, "my daughter won't listen to a word I say." Pretty soon the girl comes in and admits that she's hooked on coffee. "If I don't get a shot three times a day," she says, "I'm no better than a piece of dried-up goat meat." Papa tries to reason with her, he argues, he threatens, but nothing works until he promises to find her a handsome husband if she'll kick the habit. At last she agrees to give up the brew for a beau, but she and Bach really have the last laugh together. In a marvelous closing trio, she confides that she'll only marry a man who will let her drink all the coffee she wants.

Theory Time

All of this brings us back to our original question, which is why Bach, who worked in almost every musical form known in the 18th century, so carefully avoided opera. Well, I think it's because German opera was in such a disreputable state that he simply didn't want to have anything to do with it. Opera audiences in those days came to be seen, not to listen to the music. They would play cards, shell walnuts, chomp on oranges, and call out to friends on the other side of the theatre.[17] The singers weren't much better. While one performer was doing an aria, the others might be off on the other side of the stage arguing about something, or else they'd wander down into the orchestra to greet acquaintances. And when they did sing, they couldn't have cared less about what the composer intended. All they wanted was a chance to show off their techniques, and they were forever adding all sorts of runs and shakes and trills that weren't in the music. They also

[17]That was during the opera. Imagine what went on at intermission time.

liked to have duels with the oboe player or the flutist to see who could hold a note longer. No wonder Bach figured it would be more fun to forget about operas and remember simple things like the Saint Matthew Passion.[18]

Finale

Fortunately, Bach found enough to keep himself busy even without operas. He taught hordes of students, he inspected organs, he invented all sorts of odd musical instruments (like a lute with a keyboard, and a glockenspiel with pedals), and he composed everything from mighty masses down to cute little canons.[19] Everything he created bore the stamp of genius,[20] but along with that genius went hard work and pride. That was Johann Sebastian Bach. "This undertaking has been carried out to the best of my ability," he said about his Musical Offering. He could well have said the same thing about his whole life.

[18]The man who wrote the text for the first important musical Passion was Christian Friedrich Hunold. Two years later, he got thrown out of town for writing dirty books. You never know.

[19]Canons are just like rounds, only louder.

[20]Even some of his children.

George Frideric Handel

George Frideric Handel wrote many operas. Sometimes other composers had already written some of the music, but Handel pretended not to notice.

Early Life

Very little is known about Handel's childhood because nobody figured he would grow up to be a famous musician. We do know that the year of his birth was the same as Bach's[1] and according to one encyclopedia, his father was over sixty-one years old when he was born.[2] Papa Handel was a barber-surgeon, and not only did he dislike musicians, he refused to allow any sort of musical instrument in his house. Fortunately, Handel's mother was a more tolerant sort, and she snuck a clavichord into the attic where her husband couldn't see it.[3] Little George was delighted, and he practiced and practiced until he was a regular whiz at the keyboard.

First Chance

One day, when George was seven, he went along with his father to the Duke's Palace, and while the old man was busy

[1] It was 1685, in case you've forgotten.
[2] Which—if true—made his father the oldest baby in history.
[3] A clavichord is a very quiet instrument, so he didn't hear it either.

barbering, little George poked around until he came to a room with a shiny new organ in it. Immediately he rushed over to the instrument and started playing, louder and louder. Soon the Duke came in to see who was making all that racket. When he realized it was just a tiny child, he was so impressed that he filled George's pockets with money. He also made Papa Handel promise to give the lad music lessons.

Early Employment

So Handel studied long and hard, and after entering law school to keep his father happy,[4] he got a job as organist at the Cathedral in his home town of Halle. His next position took him to Hamburg, where he played second violin in the orchestra at the opera house near the famous Goosemarket. After that, he hoped to become chief organist of the city of Lubeck, since Buxtehude was retiring,[5] but he found out that whoever got the post would first have to marry Buxtehude's daughter. Handel took one look at her and ran right back to the opera house.[6]

Extracurricular Activities

When Handel was about nineteen, he got tired of playing second fiddle all the time and switched to first harpsichord. This was during the run of the opera *Cleopatra* by Johann Mattheson. Mattheson liked to play the harpsichord himself during the final scene, and one night Handel simply refused to let him

[4]His father had died five years earlier, but it was a nice gesture.

[5]You remember Buxtehude—he was the fellow who tried to stop Bach from being the first of the Three B's.

[6]Buxtehude spent the next three years looking for a replacement. The man he found was named Schieferdecker and he didn't play the organ too well, but I hear the wedding was very lovely.

take over. Both men could be mighty stubborn if they had a mind to, and they had minds to. Neither one would budge. They scowled at each other. Then they started shoving. Then they hauled off and began slugging. The audience immediately started watching the fight, which after all was much more interesting than the opera since nobody could tell for sure how it would come out. Even Cleopatra cheered them on. The two men fought for nearly half an hour, until at last the audience proclaimed it a draw.[7] Handel learned something very important from the whole experience, though. From then on, he stopped playing in other people's operas and started composing his own.

Success System

Handel's first opera was called *Almira,* and it contained forty-four German arias. It also had fifteen Italian arias, in case anybody didn't understand German. But it was a hit, and Handel went on to write about forty-five more operas, which is a pretty good total, considering that he also managed to compose nearly four hundred other pieces. How did he do it? Well, Handel figured out a clever little system. When he couldn't think of anything new to compose, he would take something old that he had already written and give it a new title. Or else he would use a nice tune that some other composer was finished with.[8] Sometimes he swiped whole movements at a time, but only when he was in a hurry.[9]

[7] They had even continued the battle out into the street, where Mattheson drew his sword and tried to stab Handel in the Goosemarket.

[8] Once he was caught red-handed with a theme by Bononcini, but Handel didn't care. "It was much too good for Bononcini," he said.

[9] Among the composers whose music Handel raided were Clari, Cavalli, and Carissimi. Plus Kerll, Keiser, and Kuhnau. Also Lotti, Legrenzi, Astorga, Graun, Habermann, Urio, Erba, and Porta. Oh yes, and Stradella.

Singers

Handel might have written more operas still, if he hadn't had hard times with so many of his singers. One of the wildest was named Francesca Cuzzoni. Handel sent Sandoni, the cembalo player in his orchestra, all the way from England to Italy to offer Cuzzoni a contract at a fabulous salary. She had a reputation for being stupid, stubborn, and spoiled, but she was supposed to have a glorious voice. Cuzzoni not only accepted the fee, but married the cembalo player on the way over.[10] When she arrived at the opera house, Handel realized that all those stories about her being stupid, stubborn, and spoiled were sheer truth. And then some.[11] The opera was called *Ottone,* and at the very first rehearsal Cuzzoni announced that she wasn't going to do her big aria unless Handel let her put in some extra high notes. Handel wasn't about to let her do any such thing. So they scowled at each other. Then they started shoving. It looked like the Cleopatra business all over again, except that Handel was stronger now. He seized Cuzzoni around the waist, hoisted her over a window ledge, and continued the discussion while dangling her in the air, two flights up. For some unrecorded reason, Cuzzoni suddenly decided that maybe Handel's way wasn't so terrible after all, and he set her down again. "I know that you are a witch," Handel told her, "but don't forget that I am the devil himself."

Tenor Troubles

Handel's very next opera, also produced in London, was called *Flavio Olobrio,*[12] and now that Cuzzoni was fairly well

[10]According to contemporary rumors, Sandoni later died of exposure. To some poison Cuzzoni happened to feed him.

[11]She was also short, fat, and ugly if you must know.

[12]Handel never seemed to run out of odd titles. They run from Admeto to Zenobia.

[25]

tamed, the tenor started giving him fits. His name was Gordon, and he kept complaining about the way Handel was accompanying his main aria. Needless to say, the composer was not about to change, and after one particularly heated argument the rehearsal ground to a halt. The two men scowled at each other. Then they started shoving.[13] "If you don't follow me better," Gordon screamed, "I'll jump on your harpsichord and smash it to bits." "Go right ahead," said Handel, calming down right away, "only please let me know when you'll·do it so I can

[13]See Cleopatra.

[26]

advertise. I'm sure more people will come to see you jump than to hear you sing."

Double-header

In still another opera, Handel had two prima donnas on his hands—Cuzzoni and Faustina Bordoni. Every time he wrote a nice aria for one of them, the other complained bitterly, and neither would go on with the performance until Handel had divided their parts in such a way that they had precisely the same number of lines to sing.[14] At least it was better than what happened a year later. In the middle of a performance of an opera called *Astianatte,* the two divas flew at each other right there on stage, pulling hair, smashing scenery, and bellowing some choice phrases that had escaped the librettist.[15] It may have been more fun than *Astianatte* at that.

The Highness and the Mighty

Perhaps you're wondering what Handel was doing in Britain all this time. Simple. He lived there. He was born in Germany, but he loved royalty, and Germany didn't have stately enough kings and queens to suit him. He tried Italy for a few years but it wasn't much better there, so at last Handel settled in London, and there he was happy.[16] He became Composer of Musick to the Chapel Royal, and then Composer to the Court, and soon he was writing more Royal pieces than you could shake a scepter at. He wrote a Birthday Ode for Queen Anne

[14]Their rivalry was so famous that horses named Cuzzoni and Faustina were entered in the Newmarket Races.

[15]A blow-by-blow pamphlet was published in London giving "The Full and True Account of a Most Horrible and Bloody Battle between Madame Faustina and Madame Cuzzoni."

[16]Handel always spoke English with a strong German accent, but so what? King George I didn't speak any English at all. Matter of fact, he never attended cabinet meetings because he couldn't understand what anybody was saying.

and a Wedding Anthem for the Prince of Wales and a Coronation Ode for King George II. It got so that English royalty
couldn't do a thing without Handel setting it to music.[17]

Fit for a King

Loving music was nothing new for the crowned heads of
England, of course. Edward III, who kinged around way back
in the 1370's, kept a nineteen-piece band for his royal amuse-
ment. It contained "fedelers, marver, wayghts, and cytelers,"
but since the musicians could hardly pronounce those instruments, let alone play them, the concerts were very quiet.
Edward IV added thirteen minstrels to the band. He didn't pay
them much, but every night he gave them eight gallons of ale,
so they hardly noticed. Henry VIII did even better. His court
band had seventy-nine musicians, including crumhorn players,
shawmists and sackbutters.[18]

Fit for a Queen, Too

It was Henry's daughter, Queen Elizabeth, who started the
whole business of dinner music. She simply couldn't enjoy her
supper unless a whole orchestra of fifes, kettledrums and
trumpets came by to serenade her.[19] After Elizabeth, James I
took over, and since he thought it was a pity to waste all those
instrumentalists, he hired a whole batch of composers to write
them some new music. He hired Anthony Holborne, who used
to be Gentleman Usher to Elizabeth, and he hired a guy named
Guy, and he hired Alfonso Ferrabosco II, who was left over

[17]He even wrote a lovely Funeral Ode for Queen Caroline, but she
didn't live to appreciate it.

[18]Henry was a good composer himself, and performed on several different instruments. He especially liked to play around with the virginals.

[19]Anything to take her mind off that English food.

[28]

from being Music Master to the Prince of Wales.[20] Soon, all of them were churning out reams of pieces for the King, mostly pieces for brass instruments. That way, whenever James was feeling a little out of sorts, he could just fall back on his Royal Brass.

Handel Makes a Splash

It was the great-grandson of James I who came to the English throne just when Handel was getting started in the music-for-Kings-and-Queens business. This was George I, and when he decided to go barging up the Thames one day, he naturally asked Handel to provide the music. The Master of the King's Horse took care of all the other arrangements, and on a balmy summer's evening in 1717, precisely at eight o'clock, King George set foot in his gaily decorated barge. Pretty soon he set the rest of him in there too, along with his guests, the Duchess of Newcastle, the Countess of Godolphin, and the Earl of Orkney, who was the Gentleman of the King's Bedchamber. The wife of the Master of the Horse went along too, because in her spare time she doubled as the Mistress of the King's Bedchamber.[21]

Music, Maestro

Meanwhile, over in the next barge, Handel and about fifty musicians squeezed in, set up their music stands, and began playing the famous Water Music. Side by side, the barges

[20]Alfonso Ferrabosco II was the son of Alfonso Ferrabosco I, and the father of Alfonso Ferrabosco III.

[21]Horace Walpole said that she had "two acres of cheeks, spread with crimson, and an ocean of neck that overflowed and was not distinguished from the lower part of her body." I wonder if George really knew that!

drifted peacefully down the stream, the musicians tootling away, and the King snuggling up to the Master of the Horse's wife and wondering why he had invited all those other silly people along. After an hour or so, Handel ran out of famous Water Music, but he had to do it all over again because the King was just getting in the mood. Then the tired musicians had to play it through a third time on the way back. At long last they arrived at the dock, and the King told Handel that it had been delightful, hadn't it, and that they ought to do it more often, oughtn't they. I forget precisely what Handel replied, but when George barged up the Thames again, Handel didn't contribute another drop of music.

More Operatics

After the Water Music, Handel couldn't wait to get back to writing operas again. For one big production, he imported two singers to London at his own great expense only to find that the soprano was unbelievably ugly,[22] and the mezzo had such a puny voice that he had to rewrite all the accompaniments to take away the loud instruments.[23] Later, Handel tried to write a comic opera called *Serse,* and the only funny thing about it was the lead singer, Caffarelli, who had a habit of goosing the sopranos on stage. Handel wrote one of his most glorious melodies for him—what we now know as the Largo— but the way Caffarelli sang it, it took more than a hundred years before the tune became popular.[24]

[22]She was Anna Maria Strada del Po, otherwise known as "The Pig."

[23]The mezzo-soprano was a man, incidentally. That may have been part of the problem.

[24]Some of his vocal difficulties may have been due to an unfortunate accident early in his career. His girl friend's husband came home ahead of schedule and Caffarelli had to spend the whole night hiding at the bottom of a damp well.

[30]

It was in 1749 that Handel got into another royal entangle-
ment. He was sixty-four years old then, and had just finished
his ninety-ninth cantata. Also his gout bothered him. All he
wanted to do was sit back quietly and read the funny papers.
Let somebody else write cantatas for a while. Well, wouldn't
you know it. Just when he was fixing up his pillow, in walks a
messenger from King George. Now this wasn't George I any
more, but his son, George II.[25] Anyway, the King had proclaimed a giant victory celebration and was feeling rather
pleased with himself.[26] He was going to have a few thousand
people over to the palace, the messenger said, and fireworks
in the evening and things, and would Handel please dash off
some suitable music to shoot off the fireworks by. Well, what
could Handel say? He thought of saying that he had a previous
engagement, but decided against it. You can't just go around
telling Kings of England to pop off by themselves. So, reluctantly, Handel pried himself off the pillow, and tried to think of
something that would have the proper bang.

The Big Day

Meanwhile, back at the palace, the King was turning the
affair into the biggest deal of the year. He had a huge tower
built to shoot off the fireworks from, and a huge stage built to
play the music from. He also hired a hundred and one cannons
in case the fireworks didn't make enough noise. The date was
April 21st, and there was such a crush of people trying to get
in that London Bridge was tied up for three hours. Finally,
everything was ready. King George sat down to watch on one

[25]Not that it made a whole lot of difference.

[26]England hadn't won any victories, actually, but George hated to dis-
appoint his subjects.

side of the park, and the Prince of Wales sat down to watch on the other side of the park. And there was Handel, right in the middle, ready to conduct his Royal Fireworks Music.

The Big Blow-up

Soon the fireworks started, and it was all very beautiful until the man in charge began running toward the gate. It looked terribly funny, but it wasn't. There was a fire, right in the middle of the fireworks box. You can imagine the rest. The fireworks exploded, the tower burned, the people panicked, and King George suddenly remembered that *he* had a previous engagement. So that was the end of the Royal Fireworks in the Royal Park. About the only things left intact were Handel and his Royal Fireworks Music. That's not a bad average.

Finale

Handel had ten years yet to live, and even though he was blind for most of them, and rich enough to retire, he continued to compose and perform until the very end. He wrote new arias for *Susanna* and *Solomon* to mark his seventy-fourth birthday, and on April 6th, 1759, only a week before he died, Handel conducted *Messiah* at Covent Garden. By now, he had even learned to laugh at singers he didn't hear ear-to-ear with, instead of losing his temper. One of them, named Matthew Dubourg, was always adding extra embellishments to Handel's melodies. Once, when Handel was conducting, he tried his usual stunts and got hopelessly confused, wandering farther and farther off pitch. By pure luck he managed to return to the right key, whereupon Handel, in a voice that carried through the whole theatre, roared, "Welcome Home, Mr. Dubourg!"[27]

[27]Yet Handel never held a grudge against his singers. He left Dubourg £100 in his will.

Today, more than two hundred years later, the Dubourgs and Cuzzonis and Faustinas are remembered only because their lives touched Handel's. "It is his voice," to quote Herbert Weinstock, "that remains one of the most majestic ever lifted in praise of love, of beauty, and of the art of music."

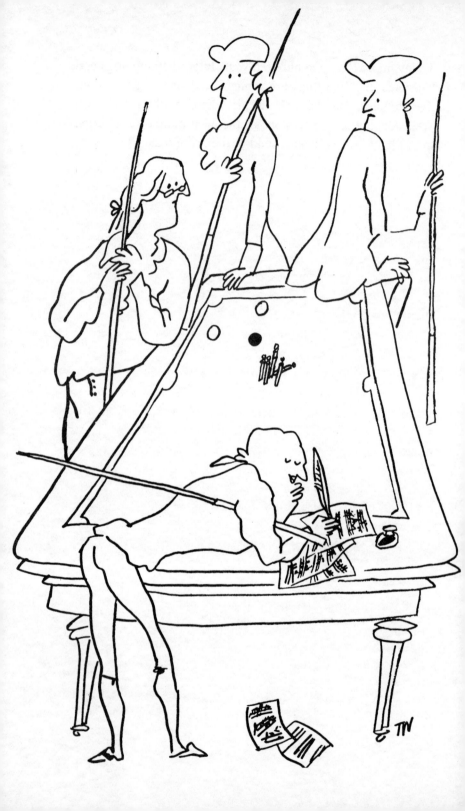

Wolfgang Amadeus Mozart

Wolfgang Amadeus Mozart honored his parents, loved his sister and adored his wife. In fact, he was such a nice fellow it's a wonder he ever amounted to anything at all.

Just Plain Folks

When he wasn't composing masterpieces, Mozart was perfectly normal. He was an atrocious speller, his math was so terrible that he couldn't even number his symphonies straight (#24 is really #31, there is no #37 at all, and so on), and he told dirty jokes.[1] Wolfgang was frightened of ghosts and trumpets, but he loved dancing, wine, and pets.[2] He was so crazy about games that he would sometimes compose pieces with a pen in one hand and a billiard cue in the other. He could also be very absent-minded. He'd forget names and places, and he took to daydreaming so much at the dinner table that his wife had to cut his meat for him, to prevent his slicing his fingers.

Head Start

Mozart was pretty sloppy, too. The manuscript of his first

[1]His father was always a little shocked, but who was he to complain? Papa Mozart wrote a whole suite called *Schlittenfahrt*.

[2]He kept a starling for three years because it learned to whistle a tune from one of his concertos.

piano concerto was so full of ink blots that his father could barely make out the notes.[3] Wolfgang would scribble numbers all over the walls and the floor and the furniture, and he refused to put his toys away unless somebody accompanied him on the fiddle. After putting up with this for a couple of years, Papa Mozart knew he had to get the kid out of the house, so he and Wolfgang went on a long series of concert tours.

On the Road

It was the same story all over Europe. Little Wolfgang charmed everybody he met with his sweet smile and his velvet coat. He was petted by every Emperor and kissed by every Empress, and he even proposed to Marie Antoinette because she dusted him off so nicely when he skidded on the slippery palace floor.[4] At the concerts, Wolfgang would play pieces using only one finger of each hand, or else he'd perform with a napkin covering the keyboard. Sometimes he made up sonatas out of tunes people sang to him, and then he'd improvise on the violin, or he'd fix up ten different accompaniments for the same aria. Once in a great while, when everybody was very tired, they actually let him play some music without any tricks attached.

Rewards

The Emperors and Empresses were so Empressed by his talents that they showered Wolfgang with gifts. Just the sort of things he always wanted, like gold toothpick-holders and silver snuffboxes and red sword-ribbons and silken kerchiefs.

[3]That's what happens when you let a four-year-old play with pen and music paper.

[4]They were both seven years old at the time, so the romance never really amounted to much.

Papa Mozart stood around trying to look pleased, but really he was going wild trying to figure out how to explain to the Emperors and Empresses that he'd rather have the cash.[5] One of the places the Mozarts liked best was England. They didn't have any Emperors and Empresses over there, of course, but Wolfgang played for King George III, and accompanied Queen Charlotte while she sang some arias, and had a marvelous time chasing their cat around the palace. Papa Mozart even considered settling down in London, but he soon changed his mind. For one thing, he couldn't stand the climate. "I must tell you," he wrote to his wife, "that there is a kind of native complaint in England which is called a 'cold.' That is why you hardly ever see people wearing summer clothes." But mainly he was worried about the loose morals. "I will not bring up my children in such a dangerous place," he said, "where the majority of the inhabitants have no religion, and where one has only evil examples before him." After England, the Mozarts went to France, Belgium, Holland, Switzerland, and Germany. All in all, they were on the road more than three years, and a most unexpected surprise came on their way back home to Austria. When the family was stopped at the border, Papa unpacked the clavichord, and little Wolfgang played on it so beautifully that the astonished officials let them pass through with all their valuable presents, duty free. "Orpheus could only tame animals with his music," boasted Papa Mozart, "but my son tamed the customs guard, and that is a great deal more difficult."

[5]Wolfgang was plagued by that sort of thing all his life. "It was just as I expected," he complained in 1777, when he was already twenty-one; "no money, only a gold watch. I now have five watches, and am seriously thinking of having an additional watch pocket sewn on each leg of my trousers, so that when I visit some great lord, it will not occur to him to present me with another."

Since Wolfgang was a little on the lazy side, he didn't start writing operas until he was twelve.[6] He also wrote an oratorio when he was eleven, but that wasn't nearly as much fun. (It was commissioned by the Archbishop of Salzburg who, suspicious that the boy might be getting outside help, locked Wolfgang up in a stuffy little room for a week, until the score was finished.) The opera Mozart completed when he was twelve was called *La Finta Semplice,* and better the Archbishop should have locked up the guy who wrote the libretto. It's about a Hungarian Captain whose Sister makes love to his Girl Friend's Brother so that the Girl Friend's Maid can marry the Captain's Valet without the Captain's Girl Friend's other Brother finding out.

And Then He Wrote

After that, Mozart composed nicer and nicer tunes for dumber and dumber stories. Like the one about a Greek shepherd who gets to choose between two goddesses, only when he picks the girl on the left, the girl on the right gets mad and throws lightning bolts at him. Or the one where the main character spends half his time hiding inside a goose.

New Development

The one thing Mozart needed more than a good libretto was a good wife. "The voice of nature speaks as loud in me as in others," he wrote his father, "louder, perhaps, than in many a big strong lout of a fellow." Wolfgang's problem, by his own admission, was that he was too much of a gentleman to seduce an innocent girl, and too much of a coward to risk catching

---

[6]Except for *Die Schuldigkeit des ersten Gebotes,* the one he composed when he was eleven, and *Apollo et Hyacinthus seu Hyacinthi Metamorphosis,* which he wrote when he was ten.

something from a non-innocent girl, and all his father could ever say was Practice, Practice, Practice. Just before his twenty-second birthday, Wolfgang finally met the girl of his dreams. Her name was Aloysia Weber, and she was sixteen and sang beautifully and even played the harpsichord a little, and it was love at first sonata. As usual, Papa Mozart was aghast at anything that might take Wolfgang's mind off his music, and he ordered his son to go off on another concert tour immediately. Rumors of the romance were still floating around when Wolfgang returned, nearly a year later, but then Aloysia became the mistress of the Elector of Salzburg, and afterwards she married an actor named Lange. That stopped the rumors. Still, Mozart had his heart set on marrying a Weber, and since there were three sisters left in the family, he moved in with all of them so he shouldn't make any mistakes this time. Eventually he picked Constanze, who was far from pretty and anything but bright and shabbily dressed most of the time. "But she understands housekeeping," Mozart explained when he wrote home asking his father's permission for the wedding.[7]

Back to Work

Now that he was a family man, Mozart realized that he'd better do something about those crummy opera plots he was being handed all the time, and he went to meet the Court Poet of Vienna to see if he could get a decent libretto out of him. The Poet pondered the predicament, and then came up with a two-act disaster called *The Husband Deceived or The Rivalry of Three Ladies for One Lover*. The main character is Sempronio the Stupid, which gives you an idea of what the plot is

[7]Wolfgang married Constanze on August 14th, 1782, without waiting for official consent, and it was just as well. Papa's permission hasn't gotten there yet.

like, and the smartest thing that Mozart ever did was to not finish composing the opera.[8]

Second Tries

Fortunately for everybody concerned, there were no hard feelings about *The Husband Deceived* because the Court Poet turned out to be quite talented after all. He was the Abbé da Ponte of Vienna,[9] and his very next collaboration with Mozart produced *The Marriage of Figaro*. After that came *Così fan tutte* and *Don Giovanni*—not a bad list for a fellow whose earlier career had been primarily noted for his knack of getting himself kicked out of some of the best cities in Italy.

Abbé Road

Da Ponte was born in 1749, seven years before Mozart, and it's hard to understand why he didn't make an opera libretto out of his own life. He wasn't too bright in school,[10] but he got to be Vice-Rector of a girls' seminary in Portogruaro, a post he held until he was tossed out for taking the title too literally. He then moved to Treviso, where he was appointed "Professore di grammatica inferiore." More than his grammar was inferior, though, and da Ponte was bounced out of there, too. Next he went to Venice, where he gambled and drank and fooled around with married women until all the husbands got together and had a law passed which said that the next time he showed his face in the city, he'd spend seven years in dun-

[8]Years later, when the Poet was writing his Memoirs, he didn't mention a word about this particular libretto. He too must have been ashamed of it.

[9]That's what he told everybody after he got through changing his name, from Conegliano, and his religion, from Jewish, and his home town, from Ceneda.

[10]He was affectionately known as "lo spiritoso ignorante."

geon. So, da Ponte moved his face to Austria, where the husbands were more tolerant. For a while, anyway. Eventually they got wise to him in Vienna too, and the Abbé had to escape to America, where he wound up running a grocery store in New York.

Juan for the Road

I mentioned earlier that Mozart liked to tell risqué stories, and now you know that da Ponte liked to live them, so it was only natural that one of their greatest collaborations should be an opera about the world's greatest scoundrel, Don Juan. According to some folks, Don Juan was a real person, a rich Spanish nobleman whose full name was Don Juan Tenorio y Salazar, but the girls never got past the Don Juan part because he was such a fast worker. If there had been tracks in the 14th century, Don Juan would have come from the right side of them. His father gave him all the best books and sent him to all the best schools, but it was no use. The only thing he ever learned to do was break women's hearts. Occasionally, the Don had to run his sword through the angry father of one of his conquests, but when the police showed up he pleaded self-defense. Finally, a group of fathers decided to save what was left of Spanish womanhood: they enticed the Don to a monastery, and there they killed him. The fathers figured they'd better have an alibi, so this time when the police appeared, they said that a stone statue had suddenly come to life and carried the Don off to the nether regions. That seemed perfectly logical, so the police closed the case, the fathers opened another one, and everybody celebrated.

Improvements

Well, that was the story, and now da Ponte was hard at work in his studio, converting it into a libretto about Don

Giovanni. He took a whole month to finish it, only it didn't seem nearly that long because there was this beautiful, sixteen-year-old girl living in the same house. Every time da Ponte felt himself slipping out of the mood (or into it), he tinkled a little bell, and in would skip the beautiful, sixteen-year-old girl. Sometimes she brought him a piece of cake, and sometimes a cup of coffee, and the rest of the time just a little inspiration. After a while, da Ponte got so inspired that he not only expanded the Don's exploits, but internationalized them, too. According to the famous "Catalogue" Aria, Giovanni had one hundred mistresses in France, two hundred and thirty-one in Germany, and six hundred and forty in Italy. There were only ninety-one in Turkey, but the list in Spain included countesses, baronesses, duchesses and several other kinds of esses, for a grand total of one thousand and three.[11]

Musical Inspiration

Well, that took care of the libretto, but Mozart still had to write the music. He moved to a little apartment near the Prague opera house to make things more convenient, but somehow he couldn't seem to get the thing finished. Every time he'd start working on an aria, somebody would invite him down to the tavern for cheese and beer, or else he'd get involved in a bowling match so that he'd only have time to scribble down a few notes between rounds. The real difficulty was that Mozart simply was too decent a fellow to know how to write nasty music about rakes and scoundrels and libertines. In fact, the whole opera might have gone right down the drain except that an old man came down to see how the rehearsals were going. It was Signor Giovanni Jacopo, Chevalier de Seingalt, otherwise known as Casanova.

[11]Those were the days!

From the Horse's Mouth

Casanova was well past his prime by now, but he had a good memory, and once he got over the shock of finding out that Mozart was writing an opera about Don Juan instead of him, he really was most cooperative. He told Wolfgang all sorts of fantastic stories about his life and loves, and believe me, Casanova had some life and loves to tell about. (They were published in twenty-eight volumes.) Anyway, he talked and talked, and told and told,[12] and he even made some corrections in the Sextet. Suddenly it dawned on Mozart that, compared to Casanova, Don Giovanni was a perfectly loveable character. Mozart could write beautiful music for his opera after all. Right away he thanked Casanova, rushed home and started composing like crazy.[13]

The Big Push

It was almost too late. The première was fast approaching, and Mozart could barely keep the singers supplied with arias in time for the rehearsals. What's more, he had to supervise the rehearsals all by himself, because da Ponte had gone back to Vienna to tinkle his bell. What a to-do. One day, Mozart had to give dancing lessons to the tenor. The next, he had a big argument with the soprano playing Zerlina because he couldn't get her to shriek loudly enough in the scene where Don Giovanni makes advances to her. Finally, he told everybody to go through the scene again, and as soon as they had started, he ran backstage, sneaked up behind the soprano and grabbed

[12]Those were the nights!

[13]Among other things, Casanova introduced the numbers racket to Paris, he was a stool pigeon for the Inquisition (spying on people's morals, yet), and he escaped from prison after having been arrested for practicing witchcraft without a license. He also played the violin, married rich widows, and wrote science-fiction stories.

her by the waist. After the shriek, Wolfgang released her, bowed gallantly, and explained: "You see, Madame, *that* is the way an innocent young woman screams when her virtue is in danger."

Saving the First for Last

The night before the première, all the arias and duets were finished at last, and the whole cast was celebrating at a big garden party. Mozart was drinking and dancing and having a great old time when the manager of the theatre rushed in with a wild look. "The overture," he yelled. "Where's the overture? It's nowhere to be found!" Oddly enough, he was right, and the reason it was nowhere to be found is that it hadn't been written yet. "Don't worry," the composer called back, thinking fast, "it's all ready." "What do you mean, ready?" the manager exploded. "Where the devil is it?" "In my head," Mozart said calmly, "all up here in my head, everything, down to the last note."

Midnight Mission

With that, Mozart scooped up a big bowl of punch and a couple of glasses, ordered the copyists to come to his apartment at seven the next morning, and went to write the overture. It was already near midnight, so Mrs. Mozart had to sit up all night with her husband, pouring him glasses of punch, and telling him stories to keep him awake.[14] But by 7 A.M., the overture was ready. Now it was the copyists' turn to work like maniacs, especially since it wasn't even that short an overture. Half an hour after the scheduled curtain time, with the orchestra men waiting, and the audience getting impatient, the music finally arrived. There was no time for rehearsal, no time even to correct the parts. The composer just looked beseechingly at the players, and gave the downbeat.

Finale

Mozart had a hard life, full of disappointments and worry, of troubles and tragedy, and, as we all know, he died pitifully young. But on the opening night of *Don Giovanni*, there was nothing but overflowing happiness in his heart. The Overture

[14]The only stories Constanze knew were things like Cinderella and Rumpelstiltzkin, so Wolfgang kept dropping off.

went perfectly, as did the opera itself. The applause swelled after every number, and by the end, the orchestra was cheering, flowers were being thrown at Wolfgang's feet, and the huge audience stood and yelled and stamped and clapped, roaring their enthusiasm in a deafening wave of sound. "My great-grandfather used to say," Mozart wrote in a letter to a friend just a few days later, "that to talk well and eloquently is a very great art, but that an equally great one is to know the right moment to stop." Mozart knew it. And I think I'll stop here, too.

P.S. Did you know that Mozart's wife, Constanze, moved to Copenhagen after his death? As a boy, I used to walk past the house she lived in, more than 150 years ago, somehow hoping I would catch a glimpse of her behind the shiny windows. In this respect, another Dane got better results. He was G. N. Nissen, and Constanze married him. They lived happily together for several years, and when Nissen died, Constanze had inscribed on his tombstone: "Here Rests Mozart's Widow's Second Spouse."

Ludwig van Beethoven

Beethoven wrote only one opera, but it seemed like more because it had two titles, three productions, and four overtures. He also wrote some incidental pieces for a couple of plays, calling them "my little operas," but he didn't fool anybody.[1]

Beginnings

Beethoven was born in 1770, and regretted it almost immediately. His grandmother was a drunken housewife, his father was a drunken choir-singer, and his mother hardly ever smiled either. As a tiny child, Ludwig showed great interest in music, picking out tunes on the piano and beginning to study the violin. It was a mistake. His father remembered the story of Mozart and how the *Wunderkind* kept getting all sorts of fancy presents, and he decided to turn Ludwig into a money-maker, too. He stood over the boy hour after hour, making him practice, and beating him up when he made too many mistakes. Some nights, the old man would be late staggering home from

[1]At least not till later, when he sold their overtures to the London Philharmonic Society, pretending they were brand new compositions.

the beer hall, but that never stopped him. He'd just wake Ludwig up and make him continue practicing.

Debut

When Beethoven was eight years old, his father arranged a big concert to show him off. Actually, Ludwig didn't play the piano all that well yet, so his father put up signs saying the lad was only six. It didn't help. People came and listened and went away again, and of the many emotions that welled up in their hearts, the most notable was complete indifference. So Ludwig's father gave up the music idea, and it's a good thing Ludwig didn't. He kept at it, and in the spring of 1787, when he was not yet seventeen, he was good enough to perform for Mozart. Mozart listened for a while, and then said, "Some day he will make a big noise in the world."[2]

[2]This probably sounds much more complimentary in German.

On the Podium

When Beethoven learned to be a conductor, he turned into one of those athletic types. He jumped up and down, and stamped his feet, and made faces and generally carried on. When he wanted the orchestra to play softly, he'd hunch way over, trying to make himself as small as possible. In pianissimo passages, he would sometimes stoop so low that he almost disappeared behind the music stand. But then another *forte* would come in the music, and Beethoven would leap wildly in the air, whirling his arms and yelling out instructions to the players. Ignaz von Seyfried, who turned pages for Beethoven at a concert in 1803, said that the master got so excited that he would often give the downbeat in the wrong place, or else he'd conduct so fast that the orchestra couldn't keep up with him.[3] When that happened, the first violinist would usually sneak up behind the podium and conduct the piece correctly. The players then watched him instead of Beethoven.

Double Trouble

Occasionally, Beethoven tried to conduct and play the piano as soloist at the same time, but that never worked out too well. For instance, at a concert in 1808. Beethoven was presenting one of his own concertos. The first time the orchestra had to play without any piano part, he jumped up to conduct and in his hurry knocked two candlesticks off the piano desk. The audience snickered, and Beethoven got so annoyed that he stopped the music and began the piece from the beginning. Also, to make sure it wouldn't happen again, he sent for two choirboys to stand next to the piano and hold the candlesticks. That worked for a while, but when that same

[3]Did you know that Beethoven was a terrible dancer? He actually couldn't stay in time with the music!

spot in the music occurred, Beethoven jumped up to conduct, and in his hurry swatted one of the choirboys, who got so frightened that he dropped the candle. This time the audience roared with laughter, and Beethoven flew into a rage. At his next solo entrance, he attacked the keyboard so furiously that half a dozen strings snapped right off.[4]

Inside Story

If you really want to know, Beethoven was terribly clumsy at home, too. He was forever dropping dishes and breaking vases and bumping into furniture, and he kept knocking his inkpot into the piano.[5] If a man ever needed a wife to take care of him, it was Beethoven. He never could remember to have the windows washed, and he always forgot to change his shirts. Once he looked so sloppy that the local policeman didn't recognize him and threw him in jail as a vagabond. Beethoven would keep a big fire roaring on warm days, and let it go out in the middle of winter. He sometimes overpaid his servants and the rest of the time he hurled books at them. But he never did get married.

Love Life

This doesn't mean that Beethoven wasn't interested in women. Quite the contrary. He had more girl friends than opus numbers. Mostly he fell in love with princesses and countesses, but when they weren't available, he settled for landladies, café-keepers, and singers. He also taught his piano students a thing

[4]Oddly enough, this was the very last concert Beethoven ever tried to conduct from the keyboard.

[5]Beethoven had an interesting habit of letting cold water pour over his hands when he was getting ready to compose. He said it helped him think.

or two.[6] Once, a fellow named Ries came over to take a lesson. and found Beethoven on the couch with the beautiful girl who had the lesson before him. He started backing out of the room, but Beethoven ordered him to the piano. "Play something sentimental," he commanded, and Ries did, his back to the couch. After a while, Beethoven called out, "Now play something passionate," and Ries did that too, kicking himself all the while for not having brought along his rear-view mirror.

More Inspirations

Beethoven saw to it that he had lots of pretty pupils. There was Giulietta Guicciardi, who preferred evening lessons. After two or three sessions, Beethoven did the honorable thing. He wrote her the "Moonlight" Sonata. He also made house calls to the Countess Anna Louisa Barbara Keglevicz,[7] and afterwards wrote her the "Amorous" Sonata. Then there was Elise Keyser. Ludwig promised her a fur-piece if she was nice, and she was nice, and he gave her "Für Elise." Beethoven also wrote a song called "The Kiss," and after a weekend or so with the Countess von Hatzfeld, he composed twenty-four variations on "Come Love."[8]

On to the Theatre

When Beethoven decided to write some substantial vocal pieces, he started by composing a Cantata on the Death of the Emperor Joseph II, and another Cantata on the Coronation of the next Emperor, Leopold II. But Leopold didn't seem to

[6]Or three.

[7]He used to come over dressed in his robe, slippers, and nightcap, so as not to waste time.

[8]Some years later, Beethoven dedicated his "Appassionata" Sonata to Count Franz von Brunswick. Hmmm!

[51]

notice, and Joseph couldn't have cared less, so Beethoven decided he would get more attention if he wrote a full-fledged opera. He began work on it in 1803, and almost immediately wished he hadn't. Nothing went right. He had to rewrite one duet eighteen times. He covered sixteen pages of notebook paper with studies for one single aria, used up another dozen trying to work up the trio. About the only nice thing was that he met a pretty young countess who loved operas, especially unfinished ones that didn't take so long to sit through. Her name was Josephine Brunswick von Deym, but Beethoven called her Pepi.[9] He would come over every other day and play her all his new arias, and then they'd go upstairs and talk about them. The opera was not getting done any faster, but it seemed more bearable, somehow.

Progress

At long last, Beethoven managed to finish the opera, except now he was nervous about the overture. He played it for some friends, and they said it was nice and everything, but since he asked, they could think of quite a few things they didn't care for. Like the whole thing. This, incidentally, is the overture we now call Leonore #1. Beethoven didn't call it Leonore #1, of course. He called it that #$%¢&$¢&#! Overture and grumpily sat down to write a new one. That one was the Leonore Overture #2, and just when Beethoven was feeling pretty satisfied, the manager of the opera house stopped by and mentioned casually that he had changed the title of the opera to *Fidelio*. Beethoven was furious, and insisted that his Overture was going to stay Leonore, no matter what. He even moved into the opera house to make sure nobody tried to pull any more fast ones during rehearsals.

[9]He said she hit the spot.

The Première

And so *Fidelio,* with its Leonore Overture, opened on November 5th, 1805, but the temperature was below zero, and all of Beethoven's friends were out of town, and the whole thing was a big flop. "It has no melodic ideas," said the critic, "and not a trace of originality—just endless repetitions and a perpetual hubbub in the orchestra."

First Aid

When the climate changed, several of Beethoven's admirers got together to try to persuade the composer to fix up some of the duller parts of the opera. Beethoven wasn't about to admit that there were any duller parts, but they served a lot of wine, and refused to feed him till afterwards, so gradually he considered some alterations. It must have been quite a scene. They went through the whole score to find the weak spots, with one singer taking all the high parts, another all the low, and a friend of Beethoven's named Franz Clement playing all the instrumental solos on the violin.[10] This went on for hours until Beethoven couldn't take it any more, and agreed to make the various cuts and changes and revisions everybody wanted. As compensation of sorts, he cut out one of the intermissions, and changed the title of the opera back to *Leonore.*

Second Aid

Only one thing remained to be done. Beethoven could hardly put out the new version of his opera with the same old overture, so he wrote a third one, better than the first and

[10]Clement had given the world première of Beethoven's Violin Concerto, but he hadn't bothered to practice it first, and he inserted one of his own novelty pieces—played on one string, with the fiddle held upside down—in between the first and second movements. Some friend.

longer than the second. It's the one containing the famous off-stage trumpet call, and the way things were going, Beethoven was lucky he didn't have the problem with it that Leopold Stokowski ran into many years later. The Maestro was conducting the Philadelphia Orchestra in this Leonore Overture #3, and both times the offstage call didn't sound on cue. As soon as the performance ended, Stokowski rushed into the wings, ready to give the delinquent trumpet player a tongue-lashing, when he found the fellow struggling in the arms of a burly watchman. "I tell you, you can't blow that damn thing in here," the watchman was saying, "there's a concert going on!"

The Second Première

In any event the new, improved Leonore opened on March 29th, 1806. It was warmer now, and Beethoven's friends were back in town, but guess who was there in the first row. The critic. "All impartial connoisseurs are fully agreed," he said, checking with his wife to make sure, "that never has anything been written so ill-knit, so disagreeable, so confused, and so revolting to the ear, with such acid modulations succeeding each other in abominable cacophony."[11] Even so, the audience seemed to like the opera, and everything would probably have worked out beautifully except that after the second night, Beethoven accused the theatre manager of holding out on his fees, which were based on a percentage of the receipts. The manager pointed out that while the loges were full, the cheaper seats had been quite empty. "I don't write for crowds," Beethoven shouted. "I write for musicians." "So don't complain about the fees," the manager snapped back, sending Beethoven off into one of his furies. "Return the score to me at

[11]The curtain hadn't even gone up yet, mind you. He was still talking about the overture.

once!" he thundered, and when the manager complied, Beethoven stalked out with it, absolutely forbidding any further performances. And so, *Leonore* went back on the shelf, and stayed there for eight long years.

Music Incidentally

Having sworn off operas for the time being, Beethoven decided to write some incidental music instead. Normally he didn't do this because he couldn't see why his music should be incidental to anything. On the other hand, if Beethoven was short of cash, he'd write all the incidental music anybody wanted to pay for. One day in 1811, when Beethoven was fresh out of money, a Hungarian playwright came to see him. His name was August Friedrich Ferdinand von Kotzebue, which was a bad sign already. Kotzebue had written a play called *The Ruins of Athens,* to help celebrate the opening of a new theatre in Pest,[12] and he wanted Beethoven to compose the incidental music for it. Beethoven looked at Kotzebue's play, and it was the second worst play he had ever read. The first worst was Kotzebue's other play, *King Stephen, Hungary's First Great Benefactor,* and Beethoven was supposed to write incidental music for that one also.[13]

The Plot Thickens

To get back to *The Ruins of Athens,* you can't possibly imagine how ridiculous the story is. It's all about Minerva and Mercury, two Greek gods who have a hard night on Olympus

[12]This was before Buda joined Pest.

[13]Kotzebue had written a third play, even worse than the other two, called *Bela's Escape,* but the Emperor cancelled it. It seems he had spent the better part of two years escaping from the French army, and he didn't want any wise remarks from the audience.

and lie down for a two-thousand-year snooze. When they get up, they stretch, and then go down to see how Athens is doing after all that time. They should have stayed in bed another couple of thousand years. Athens is a mess. Then they go over to see how Rome is doing. Rome is even a bigger mess than Athens. Then they look over the whole wide world, and they discover that in the whole wide world, the only really decent place left is the city of Pest, under the magnificent rule of the Great and Glorious Emperor Franz, Long Live the Great and Glorious Emperor Franz, Rah! Rah! Rah![14] Beethoven wrote and delivered the music, including the famous Turkish March, and then went home feeling miserable for having sunk so low. When he got there, he found the check, and felt elevated right away.

Symphonies

Just when Beethoven was figuring that maybe he'd better forget about stories and stick to symphonies, along came Johann Nepomuk Maelzel. Maelzel was even more of a character than Kotzebue. He didn't write things, he invented them. He invented a mechanical bugler that played flat, and he invented an automatic chess player that kept losing,[15] and he invented an ear trumpet that didn't hear very well. He also invented the metronome, which worked beautifully, but that was an accident. One day, Maelzel invented the biggest contraption of his career. It was called the Panharmonicon, and it was something like a gigantic music box, run by air pressure. It was able to reproduce perfectly the sounds of all the instru-

[14]Emperor Franz was paying for the whole thing, so Kotzebue figured it was the least he could do.

[15]Napoleon played a game with the machine once and beat it hands down. The machine worked on a novel principle, by the way: inside it a man was hidden, telling the thing what to do.

ments, Maelzel said, and all that was needed to make both him and Beethoven rich was a new symphony for the machine to play at a benefit concert.[16]

Music with a Bang

Beethoven was much too smart to spend a lot of time thinking up themes for a machine symphony, so he worked out a short cut. It so happened that only a few months earlier, the English had defeated the French in Spain, and that, he decided, is what he'd describe in his music. He picked an English folk tune to represent the English Army, and a French folk tune to represent the French Army, and then he stuck in both tunes at the same time to represent the Battle. Later, he played "God Save the King" louder than everything else, which meant that the piece was over and the English had won again. By the time the symphony was completed, the Panharmonicon was out for repairs, so Beethoven had to rescore the whole thing for regular orchestra. Fortunately, he threw in a few cannon shots and musket firings to make the battle parts more realistic, and the audience went wild with excitement. They cheered and whistled and demanded encores. In fact, the Battle Symphony did more to make Beethoven famous and popular than any other piece he had ever written, because even if it wasn't his best composition, it certainly made the biggest noise. Mozart was right, after all!

Leonore Again

The enormous success of the Battle Symphony had one excellent side effect. It made Beethoven such a big shot that a Viennese impresario decided to revive his opera, *Leonore*.

[16]Beethoven didn't care for benefit concerts as a rule, but Maelzel explained that this one would be for their own benefit, so he went along with the idea.

[58]

Once again, Beethoven fumed and fussed with dozens of changes. Scenes were shifted, new arias written, settings revised. Then, at the last moment, when everything was all ready to go, Beethoven decided that he couldn't stand the thought of putting out his new version of the opera with the same old overture. Quickly he set to work, but he was so exhausted that he didn't quite make it. The impresario came to his room on the morning of the première, and there was Beethoven, fast asleep at his workbench, with unfinished pages strewn about the floor, and remnants of his supper on the table: zwieback dipped in wine.[17] As a result, the impresario had to use another Beethoven overture left over from a concert a few years earlier, and he was so annoyed about it that he took out a big red crayon and changed the title of the opera back to *Fidelio*. By now Beethoven was tired of fighting, so when he finished the Overture a few days later, he called it *Fidelio* as well. To everybody's astonishment, the critic stayed home, and both the opera and its Overture were a tremendous success.

Happy Ending

Beethoven was so elated that he immediately laid plans to compose another opera. He even asked Kotzebue to write him a libretto about Attila the Hun. But Kotzebue was busy,[18] and Beethoven didn't like any of the other plots he read, and mainly he started thinking back to those sixteen pages in the notebooks, and the four Overtures and the critic in the first row, and the winy zwieback, and he decided not to bother. And he didn't.

[17]Have you ever tried zwieback dipped in wine? No wonder Beethoven couldn't finish the overture!

[18]He was shot by a German student in 1819. The police said the student was a radical, but considering the quality of Kotzebue's work, perhaps the fellow was merely a literature major.

Gioacchino Rossini

Gioacchino Rossini was born in 1792, five months after his parents got married, and it taught him a lesson. He was never early for another appointment in his whole life. Rossini was the laziest boy in town. He even became the laziest man in town. But that was later. He also managed to be born on February 29th, which he considered a good break, because he didn't have to bother with so many celebrations.[1]

All in the Family

Rossini's father combined jobs as Municipal Trumpeter and Inspector of Public Slaughterhouses, so Gioacchino grew up liking horns and bologna. Luckily, his mother was a singer, so Gioacchino grew up liking operas, too. When Rossini's father wasn't trumpeting in town, he was travelling all around the country, playing in local bands and theatres. Since Mama Rossini was out on the road a lot also, Gioacchino was often left with his grandmother.

Childhood

She found that Gioacchino was like any other boy, except lazier. He wouldn't study, he wouldn't work, and he hated to practice. His tactics drove his first piano teacher to drink,

[1]On his eighteenth birthday, he was already seventy-two!

which really wasn't that difficult since the teacher, whose name was Prinetti, manufactured brandies on the side. Prinetti liked to go to sleep standing up in a corner of the room, all wrapped in a cloak, and when he woke up, he made Rossini play scales using only his thumbs and index fingers. Actually, the things Gioacchino liked best were throwing stones at his playmates and cracking jokes in church. As punishment, he had to pump bellows for the local blacksmith. That he hated even more than practicing.

Music at Last

Eventually, his grandmother had enough of all this, and Gioacchino was boarded out with a pork butcher in (here it is again) Bologna. He still didn't take music seriously, but one day the butcher decided it was about time the kid did some work around the place. Suddenly, Gioacchino became terribly interested in music, and announced that he couldn't do any work around the place because he was too busy studying to be a boy soprano. That worked pretty well until his voice changed. Then Rossini chose composing as a career, since he found he could do it in bed.

Bedside Manner

My favorite bedroom story about Rossini dates from many years later. He was snuggled under the blankets writing a duet for an opera when the page slipped out of his hand and fell under the bed. Since he was too lazy to get up and fetch it, he simply took another sheet and composed an entirely new duet. Later, when a friend stopped by and retrieved the music for him, Rossini couldn't bear the thought of letting all that energy go for nothing, so he added an extra part on the page, turning the duet into a trio for the same opera. Speaking of operas, Rossini wrote a whole lot of them, but that was only so he could make enough money to stay in bed and not write operas any more. When he was thirty-seven, he reached his goal. For the next forty years, everybody kept waiting for Rossini to break down and compose another opera, but he never did. He was much too happy in bed.[2]

First Flings

It would only be fair to tell you about some of the operas that Rossini did write. The first one came along when he was eighteen, and it was about the love life of a girl named Fanny Mill. (A couple of letters up the alphabet, and he'd have had a smash hit. As it was, some people complained that Rossini had done too much research for the romantic duets.) His second opera was even more daring. It told of a suitor who gets rid of his rival by convincing him that the lady they admire is really a castrato in disguise. The police closed that one down after three performances.[3] Rossini's third opera was produced in Venice, where the police were more lenient, and when it was over somebody let loose an enormous flock of doves, canaries, and wild pheasants from one of the loges. Rossini took it as a compliment, which was probably just as well.

On and Upwards

As his operas improved and Rossini became more popular, requests for new productions started coming in from all over Italy. Gioacchino would much rather have stayed in bed, of

[2]He did write a piece called "Miscarriage of a Polish Mazurka," and one called "Profound Sleep with Startled Awakenings" and even a "Hygienic Prelude for Morning Use," but no more operas.

[3]They would have moved in sooner, but the Chief had to see it several times to get the point.

course, but he needed the money, so he churned out dozens of operas, often swiping arias from one work to fit the next. What really annoyed him was having to write double endings. With *Tancredi,* for instance, people complained that the sad scenes were spoiling their digestion, and the manager wouldn't leave Rossini alone until he had written a last-minute reprieve for the hero. The same thing happened with *Otello.* The audience began whooping and yelling as soon as the last scene started, trying to warn Desdemona to beat it before Othello finished her off. They kept it up night after night, until Rossini had to create a whole new finale where the lovers kiss and make up.

Under and Overtures

If anything gave Rossini more headaches than the endings, it was the beginnings. Whenever he could, he simply dusted off an old overture and added the title of the new opera. Most impresarios were wise to him, though, and demanded their money's worth. With *The Thieving Magpie,* Rossini waited until the very day of the première. Then he came down to the opera house, smiling and cheerful, saying to the manager what a nice idea it would be to have an opera without an overture for a change. Especially since he hadn't written it yet. Unfortunately, the manager didn't think it was a nice idea in the least.[4] What's more, he locked Rossini up in the attic of the opera house with pen, paper and four husky stagehands. The pen and paper were for Rossini to write *The Thieving Magpie* Overture with, and the four husky stagehands were for throwing him out the window in case he didn't. So he did. As fast as he could dash off the pages, Rossini flung them through the window. Below, in the courtyard, a small army of copyists

[4]In fact, he thought it was the worst idea he'd heard in years.

scooped them up and wrote out the parts for the orchestra, while the impatient impresario danced around tearing his hair. "All my impresarios were bald at thirty," Rossini boasted when he finished the job, just barely in time for the opening.[5]

Personal and Confidential

In 1815, Rossini went to Naples, where an impresario named Barbaia needed some new operas to occupy the early evenings of his leading prima donna, Isabella Colbran.[6] Rossini came through with several operas almost on schedule. Then, mumbling something about Barbaia looking tired lately and maybe needing more rest, he ran off with Isabella. Gradually he married her, and they were very happy together until Rossini began to notice that he was even happier when they weren't together. One day he walked out of the house, saying he'd be right back. Which he was, nearly four years later. Meanwhile, Rossini was getting very friendly with a pretty Parisian named Olympe Pélissier. Once he brought Olympe home to Isabella for lunch, just to show that there were no hard feelings.[7]

Fame and Fortune

All this time, Rossini was getting more and more famous. In 1823, he figured out that twenty-three of his operas were being played in various parts of the world, including the Middle East, where one potentate couldn't enjoy his breakfast unless a brass band played Rossini tunes outside his window. Even after he retired, Rossini could hardly keep track of all

[5]Rossini himself used to wear two or three wigs, one on top of the other, so he wouldn't have to bother taking the bottom ones off.

[6]Barbaia had already figured out how to take care of her late evenings.

[7]That day he definitely should have stayed in bed.

the honors that came pouring in. The Sultan of Turkey bestowed upon him the Order of Micham-Iftihar, and a sausage maker in Modena sent along some zamponi and cappelletti. He got a ribbon from the King of Sweden and a snuffbox from the Czar of Russia. In London, King George invited Rossini down to the palace to sing duets, and in Madrid, King Ferdinand offered him the bottom half of a cigar he had been smoking. In Paris, King Charles named Rossini Inspector General of Singing in France. (Nobody knew what that was supposed to mean, but since the title included a handsome salary, Rossini felt that he ought to be doing something to earn it. The best he could come up with was wandering around Paris, inspecting the songs of street beggars and drunks.) On his 70th birthday,[8] a group of friends arrived with a surprise announcement: they had collected twenty thousand francs to erect a Rossini monument. "What a waste of money," the composer groaned. "Give me the cash, and I'll stand on the pedestal myself!"

Roadblocks

Despite all this, Rossini's journey to immortality was not without its share of detours. Several of his efforts were hissed off the stage, and on one occasion Rossini sent a wordless review of his latest production to his mother: a drawing of a large, straw-covered bottle—the kind Italians call a fiasco. But most devastating of all was the scalping that originally greeted Rossini's comic masterpiece, *The Barber of Seville*.

Prelude

It all began when Rossini accepted a commission to write an opera for the Roman carnival celebrations of 1816. His

[8]He was now seventeen and a half. See Leap Year.

contract specified that he would compose the music, adapt it to suit the convenience of the singers, preside at all rehearsals, and conduct the first three public performances from the keyboard. For this he would be paid four hundred scudi and given a brass-buttoned suit to wear at the première.[9] Well, no sooner had Rossini signed on the dotted line than the impresario came over and said that by the way he had forgotten to mention that the Roman carnival came early that year, and could he please have the opera in three weeks because otherwise Rossini wasn't going to get the scudi *or* the suit.

Panic Button

Most composers in that sort of situation would have become hysterical, but Rossini just shrugged. *Then* he became hysterical. Tossing aside the libretto that had originally been given him, he rushed to the library and took out a famous play that had previously been made into operas by at least half a dozen other composers. It was Beaumarchais' *The Barber of Seville*.[10] Rossini next converted his house into a music factory. He sat writing at the piano in one room, with his librettist spewing out verses in the next, and copyists lining the corridors working out the parts. As soon as the ink was dry, the pages were sped to the singers, who were rehearsing upstairs.

Simple Little System

Remember how Handel solved similar problems? Rossini also knew perfectly well that he could never compose an en-

[9]A scudo, as any 19th-century Italian can tell you, was worth about $.97.

[10]Please remind me to tell you about Beaumarchais, sometime. He made clocks, smuggled guns, stole state secrets, and married rich widows who died a few months afterwards, accidentally.

tirely new opera in such a short time, so he surrounded himself with all the music he had ever written. He pored over his sketchbooks, and stormed through his earlier operas, particularly the flops, which people wouldn't remember. Then, like a scavenger, he swooped down, lifting a march tune here, a largo there, here a chorus, there an aria. When he couldn't find anything of his own that he liked, he borrowed a few tunes by other composers. Finally the job was done. Out of bits and pieces of a dozen old scores, Rossini had created a fresh, brilliantly exciting new one. During those three weeks, he had not left the house, he had hardly taken time to eat, and he had grown a wild black beard. In more ways than one, Rossini was now ready for the Barber.[11]

Another Close Shave

As usual, Rossini waited until the day before the première to write the overture, which was to be based on Spanish folk tunes, and just when it began to look as if he really would have to sit down and compose it, he got a brilliant idea. He rushed around telling everybody that he had written the most masterful overture of his career, only it had mysteriously disappeared. They searched like crazy all over the place, but naturally the music never turned up. So Rossini happily went back to his trunk and got out a brand old overture he had written some years earlier for an opera about a Greek emperor. When that flopped, Rossini had used the same music as the overture to another opera, about an English queen. That one didn't do too well either, but Rossini was a hard man to discourage. He crossed off the two other titles, wrote "Barber of Seville Overture" in capital letters, and lay down for a quick nap.

[11]When Donizetti heard that Rossini had completed the whole opera in three weeks, he just shook his head. "Yes, yes," he said, "Rossini always was a lazy fellow."

More Problems

The score may have been finished, but Rossini's troubles were only beginning. I mentioned that other composers also had used the same story for their operas. Well, one of them was still around. His name was Giovanni Paisiello, and his *Barber of Seville* had been quite successful about thirty-four years earlier. When Paisiello heard that Rossini was trying to top him, he was furious. He announced that Rossini was "a licentious composer who paid little attention to the rules of his art, a debaser of good taste, and a man whose great facility results only from a good memory."[12]

Opening Night

When the night of the première arrived, Paisiello stayed home sulking. But he sent a group of friends to the theatre to carefully organize a whole series of spontaneous demonstrations during the performance. His people hooted and laughed and hissed and yelled, until the singers hardly could hear the orchestra. Naturally, the performers got rattled. Almaviva neglected to tune his guitar for the Serenade to Rosina, and while he was monkeying with the pegs, a string snapped in his face. Don Basilio came out and immediately tripped over his costume. Another singer fell through a trap door, scenery toppled over, and during the finale of the first act somebody let a cat loose on the stage. The opera was a shambles, and Rossini went home in despair.[13]

[12]Rossini tried to smooth things over by changing the name of his opera to *The Useless Precaution*, but it proved to be just that. Paisiello was still furious.

[13]They say that Rossini only wept three times in his life: once when he heard a fellow composer sing, once after the première of *The Barber of Seville,* and the third time at a picnic when the truffled chicken fell into the river.

Happy Ending

Fortunately, Paisiello was satisfied with reports of the wreckage, and his friends stayed away from the second performance.[14] Without the distractions, the audience loved the show, and on the third night, the cheering crowd gave the composer a festive, torchlight procession, escorting him all the way back to his lodgings. Within a few years, Rossini's *Barber* had become one of the most popular operas in the world. It was given in Russia (in Russian), in France (in French), in England (in English), in Germany (in German), in Denmark (in Danish). Also in America (in Italian).

Golden Years

So, finally, Rossini retired, and instead of writing operas, he presided over the greatest series of musical soirées ever held in Paris. Liszt, Rubinstein, Saint-Saëns, Gounod, all were proud to be included on the guest-artist list, and every so often, the old man himself would perform a couple of his latest compositions on the piano. At this point, Rossini's pieces had titles like "Anchovies," "Radishes" and "Hors d'Oeuvres," and they were all very short because he couldn't wait for supper time.

Medical Report

Speaking of food, Rossini was a renowned gourmet, an extraordinary cook, and he ate so much that he grew incredibly fat. Never mind the radishes, he would wolf down enormous portions of cambelloni, sausages, cheese, ham, paté and stuffed pasta. Then he wondered why his stomach was always upset. "I have all of woman's ills," he complained, "all that I lack is a uterus." When he wasn't sick from his illnesses, Rossini suf-

[14]So did Rossini. He called in sick.

fered from his cures, which included everything from leeches to warm baths.[15] On two occasions, newspapers reported that he had died, and Rossini almost agreed with them.

Personal Report

But he kept smiling. In fact, Rossini's sense of humor never dimmed. When Gilbert-Louis Duprez, a famous tenor, came over to the house and proudly sang his high C, Rossini's only reaction was to rush over to see if any of his valuable Venetian glass had been shattered. Another tenor, named Enrico Tamberlik, boasted that he could go even higher, and Rossini instructed his butler to show the fellow in. "But tell him to leave his C-sharp on the coat rack," he added; "he can pick it up again when he leaves." When Meyerbeer died, Rossini had another visitor—the late composer's nephew, who had written a funeral march and insisted on playing it. "Very nice," Rossini growled after the performance, "but wouldn't it have been much better if *you* had died and your uncle had composed the march?"

Farewell

Even in his final great composition, the "Petite Messe Solenelle," Rossini had his little jokes. For one thing, the Mass is neither little nor solemn. For another, he directed that it be sung by "twelve singers of three sexes." Rossini also wrote an open letter to accompany the work. "Dear God," it said, "here it is, my poor little Mass, done with a little skill, a bit of heart, and that's about all. Be Thou blessed, and admit me to Paradise."

I bet Rossini made it.

[15]One of his prescriptions blended mallow, gum and oil of sweet almond. Another contained flower of sulphur mixed with cream of tartar.

Hector Berlioz

The life of Hector Berlioz is recommended for mature adults only, although no one would dare make a movie out of it. Berlioz lived right in the middle of the romantic era, and he didn't forget it for a minute. "My arteries quiver violently," he wrote in his *Memoirs*, "my muscles contract spasmodically, my limbs tremble, my feet and hands go numb." That was from listening to music. Wait till you hear what happened when he found out about girls.

Beginnings

Berlioz was born on December 11th, 1803. His father, the Doctor, was wise and learned, although not enough to cure his own stomach trouble. He was the author of a book on cupping and acupuncture, and couldn't understand why his son didn't want to follow in his footsteps and become a doctor. Hector understood perfectly well. He would have been perfectly willing to follow his father in his footsteps, he just didn't want to become a doctor. He was fascinated by all sorts of odd things,[1] only medicine didn't happen to be one of them.

Musical Beginnings

His musical career started one day when he was rummaging

[1] He could name every one of the Sandwich Islands.

around in a drawer at home, and found a little toy flute. He piped at it for hours, until his father couldn't stand it any more and taught him how to *play* the thing. Later, little Hector brought a drum home from school and pounded it for hours, until his father couldn't stand *that* any more and bought him a guitar.

Passionate Beginnings

It was about this time that Hector's romantic personality began to assert itself. "I felt my heart swell," he said, "my budding imagination opened wide, my lips trembled, my voice faltered and broke, I was seized with a nervous shuddering." This was from reading the *Aeneid*. He still hadn't found out about girls. That notable event occurred when Hector was twelve, and eighteen-year-old Estelle Gautier came to spend the summer near by. She was tall, shapely, beautiful, had a dazzling smile, and she wore pink boots. Hector had never seen pink boots before, so he fell madly in love with her. He cowered in terror when she looked his way, and he screamed in rage when she danced with another man. He couldn't eat or sleep, and spent hours lying in the corn field, secretly watching her, and daydreaming about her charms.[2] That's how it went, week after week, all through the summer.

Music Again

After Estelle had left, Berlioz discovered that music was the only cure for a broken heart, and he started composing. Mostly he wrote sad songs about unrequited love, but he also composed despairing melodies to poems about a shepherdess named Estelle, and he started working on a tragic opera called *Estelle*. He never finished the opera and he destroyed the love

[2]For variety, he would spend a few hours lying in the orchard.

songs, but at least he wasn't lying around corn fields any more. As Hector got more and more involved with music, his father got more and more upset with him, because that was no way to become a doctor. Papa yelled and pleaded, and casually left enticing anatomy pictures lying about the house. But Hector simply wasn't interested . . . until one day the Doctor offered to buy his son a shiny new flute, with all the latest keys, if only he'd settle down and study osteology. Hector agreed, and when the shiny new flute came, he felt pretty good about the whole thing. But after that, he looked in the dictionary, and found that osteology is a study of the features comprised in the bony structure of an organism or any of its parts.

Seeing the City of Light

You know what they say about clouds. The silver lining to Berlioz' medical career was the fact that the school was located in Paris, the city of gorgeous women and lavish opera. Matter of fact, the second thing Hector did in Paris was go to the opera houses. For more than a year, he kept his bargain and attended medical school regularly.[3] But with music foremost on his mind, he would sing arias in the dissecting room,[4] and copy opera scores instead of doing his Experimental Electricity homework. Naturally, his emotions were still easily aroused. "I was filled with fearful agitation," he wrote about one evening at the theatre. "I could feel my heart beating violently, I blushed scarlet, there was a buzzing in my ears, I felt dizzy." That was when he went backstage to visit an actor. Wait till you hear what happened when he visited actresses.

[3]Though his heart was still in the houses of Paris.

[4]His favorite was "Descend into the Sea-Nymph's Breast," which is from Salière's *The Danaïds*.

[75]

After another year of osteologizing more and enjoying it less, Berlioz finally gave up medicine for good, and entered the famous Paris Conservatory of Music. He also started composing again. He wrote a Cantata about a horse, an Oratorio about an ocean, an Opera about a gambler, and a Mass about children. When he finished, he brought them over to some friends, and asked for their honest opinions. Soon he made a big fire and burned a Cantata, an Oratorio, an Opera and a Mass.

Meanwhile, Dr. Berlioz was so indignant about all this that he cut off his son's allowance.[5] To make ends meet, Hector had to take a job singing in the chorus of a vaudeville theatre, and another one writing articles for a local paper. Still, there were the enticements of Paris. "My brain seemed ready to burst," Berlioz wrote, "my blood was on fire, I felt as if burning embers were scorching my veins, I tore my hair and wept, I beat with my fists against my skull." That was when he had to write an opera review. He still hadn't met any actresses.

On Stage

The big moment arrived on October 11th, 1827. Berlioz went to see Shakespeare's *Hamlet*, with an Irish girl named Harriet Smithson starring as Ophelia. Harriet spoke with a heavy Irish brogue, and she forgot her lines in the middle of the mad scene, rushing off the stage in tears. Hector didn't understand even one word of English, and thought it was all part of the show. It was love at first sight, the sort of wild, passionate love that could only happen to Berlioz. "A lightning flash of discovery revealed the whole heaven of art," he wrote, "illuminating it to its remotest corners. I recognized

[5]Fortunately for Hector, his father was not a surgeon.

the true meaning of beauty. I saw, I understood, I was alive at last." That's what he said about Shakespeare. I wouldn't dream of repeating what he said about Harriet.

Encore

The very next day, Berlioz was back in his seat to see Harriet in *Romeo and Juliet,* and his doom was sealed even more tightly. On the spot, he vowed to marry her, and to compose his greatest piece in her honor. The only hitch was that Harriet was much too famous to bother with unknown French composers, especially poor ones. Hector wrote her long, gushy love letters, and she wouldn't open them. He arranged a concert of his music to impress her, and she wouldn't attend it. Once he made up his mind to go backstage and declare his passion in person. When he got there, she was rehearsing a love scene. Berlioz took one look at her, gave a bloodcurdling shriek, and ran out into the street in a fit of jealousy.[6]

Aftermath

Berlioz was in a bad way now. Every time he saw Harriet's picture on a poster, he nearly went out of his mind. He took to wandering about Paris in a daze, and sometimes in the nights too. He started lying around corn fields again, chewing stalks of grass when he got hungry, and sleeping anywhere he happened to doze off—alongside the Seine, in a snow bank, even on a tabletop in a busy café.[7] At last he remembered how music could cure a broken heart, and he started composing his *Symphonie Fantastique,* which by some strange coincidence is about a beautiful girl who spurns a sensitive young musician

[6]"Watch out for that fellow with the crazy eyes," said Harriet (*"dont les yeux n'annonçaient rien de bon"*), and went back to kissing Romeo.

[7]The waiters would tiptoe around him, afraid he might be dead.

and drives him to some bad opium trips. In his music, the jealous composer portrayed Harriet as everything from an evil temptress to an ugly witch. He also added insult to inference by representing her with one of the tunes he had originally written to express his love for Estelle and her pink boots. Secretly, Berlioz hoped that Harriet would hear about his symphony, and be so ashamed of herself that she'd come rushing into his arms forever.

After the Aftermath

It was a good idea, but it didn't work. The Fantastic Symphony was played with some success, but by that time Harriet had left France to continue her tour, and Hector was even more miserable than before. His friends were terribly worried and did everything they could to console him, but nothing helped. Not until a pretty young piano teacher decided to try out her own method. Her name was Marie-Félicité-Denise Moke, but Berlioz called her Camille because he was in a hurry. Soon Camille and Hector were engaged, and everything was looking up again.[8]

Complications

At just about this time, on August 21st, 1830, Berlioz won the Prix de Rome, meaning that he went off to study in Italy for a couple of years, while Camille waited patiently in Paris for him to return. After a couple of months, Camille's patience ran out and she decided to get married right away. To somebody else. "I suffered agonies," wrote Berlioz, "I lay groaning on the ground, stretching out abandoned arms, convulsively tearing off handfuls of grass. I felt as though my heart were

[8]Camille smoked big, strong cigars, and she thought Beethoven's andantes were too long, but Hector wanted to marry her anyway.

evaporating and about to dissolve, my skin burned all over my body." That was when he was longing for Paris. When he heard how Camille was being consoled by a new lover, he really got upset.

Revenge

Hector's first impulse was to throw himself into the ocean, but after he actually did it he discovered he couldn't swim. So he gave up that idea and hatched a much more impressive plan. He bought himself a chambermaid's dress, complete with hat and veil, a pair of loaded pistols, and two bottles of poison. The plot was for him to go to Paris, enter Camille's house disguised as a maid, and shoot her and her boy friend right in the middle of a consolation. The poison was in case the guns didn't work. Berlioz was quite pleased with the disguise,[9] and without waiting another day he took the first coach for Paris.

More Complications

If it wasn't one thing, it was another. First, Berlioz took the wrong coach by mistake and wound up in Genoa instead of Paris. Then, when he got out, he left his disguise behind, and had to waste a whole afternoon looking for a seamstress who could sew him another one. After the delay he boarded another coach, not realizing that that one wasn't going to Paris either. It went to Nice, and it was so nice in Nice that Hector decided to stay and forget the whole business. He sold the pistols and looked around to see who could console *him* for a while. Later, Berlioz admitted that this was the happiest month of his whole life. He spent hours lying in the orange groves, and climbing over cliffs, and dozing in the heather. He might have stayed

[9]"You're charming," said the cashier when he tried on the dress, so Hector left the girl a twenty-franc tip.

indefinitely except that the police ran him out of town as a suspicious character.[10]

Back to Normal

Berlioz returned to Rome and finished his Italian studies without further excitement. On the side, he attended a lot of operas, and read a lot of poetry. He also decided to write some operas himself. With the first couple, he couldn't even get past the overture. The third time, he started in the middle, but that wasn't much of an improvement. It just meant he didn't get to the overture at all. "I wept and collapsed," said Berlioz, "my heart dilated, I existed in a kind of frenzy, with floods of tears and uncontrollable sobbing." That was when he was still reading poetry. He planned to take care of the opera problem when he got back to Paris.

The First Opera

When the time came to leave Rome, Berlioz was delighted. He absolutely hated the place and couldn't wait to get out. He called it "a stupid town" because nobody there wanted to hear his music.[11] Still, he wasn't about to throw away all that hard-earned local color, so when he returned to France and really composed an opera all the way through, he made it about the Italian sculptor Benvenuto Cellini, and gave it a Roman setting.

The First Fiasco

No sooner did he write this big, long opera about Benvenuto Cellini than Berlioz began rehearsing it to death. By

[10]Amazing how they could tell.

[11]Why pick on Rome? People didn't want to hear his music in lots of towns.

[80]

run-through #29, the conductor couldn't bear the music any longer, the orchestra members were so bored that some were caught playing folk tunes instead of the written parts in the finale, and the male dancers kept pinching the females until the girls were outshrieking the chorus. Then came opening night, and when the opera was over, everybody in the audience agreed. It was terrible.

Salvage Job

Recovering from the sting, Berlioz combined three or four of the tunes the audience hated most into a Concert Overture. Surprise! The people hissed and booed like anything. At last it dawned on him what the trouble was. The title. Who wanted to hear an overture about some old sculptor who hadn't sculpted anything for four hundred years? Sure enough, Berlioz crossed out *Benvenuto Cellini,* wrote *Roman Carnival* instead, and the music became a tremendous hit. To quote one review, "Its fire, precision, vivacity and vehemence have the effect of a fireworks display. It contains a variety of ideas, an energy and exuberance and a brilliance of color such as I may never hear again." Berlioz would have made his review even more glowing, but modesty prevented him.

Juliet Again

Just when everything seemed to be going nicely for a change, Harriet Smithson returned to Paris. Berlioz wasn't nearly so unknown any more, so this time Harriet came to one of his concerts. Hector was playing tympani that day, and as soon as she arrived in the hall, his kettledrums boiled over. For the rest of the piece, every time her eyes met his, he thwacked the drums as hard as he could. This was a little confusing in the places where there was no kettledrum part, but Berlioz

didn't care. At last he met the girl of his dreams, and within a few months he proposed to her. Harriet turned him down at first, but Hector pleaded and pestered, and then he swallowed some poison right in front of her to prove that his intentions were honorable. Eventually she gave in, and Hector and Harriet were married on October 3rd, 1833. Six years later, it was 1839. That year, Berlioz wrote a great piece of music in her honor, making the second part of his youthful vow come true.

R & J

This was *Romeo and Juliet*. By the time he got ready to work on it, Harriet had turned into a nagging, jealous wife. But Hector could still remember the good old days when he was tearing his hair out and sleeping in the snow, so he wasn't too upset. A bigger problem was that he couldn't figure out whether *Romeo and Juliet* should be an *opera* without action or a *symphony* with singing. Now and then it seemed to be turning into a *cantata,* which didn't seem appropriate at all. Meanwhile, the darn thing was getting bigger and bigger, until it ended up being scored for two hundred instrumentalists, three vocal soloists and a huge chorus. Not bad for some music about a couple of mixed-up 14th-century teenagers.[12] Not that the critics liked it: "a ridiculous little noise, reminiscent of badly oiled syringes," one reviewer called it. Berlioz replied that the critic was "full of crapulous stupidity."

[12]In Verona, you can still see the balcony where Juliet made her famous scene, and the chapel where she married Romeo. At least that's what the guidebooks say. There's also a cute little letter box right outside the chapel through which the spirit of Juliet gives advice to the lovelorn.

If you have a romantic problem, you leave a note in the box, and eventually you get an answer from an anonymous city official known as Juliet's Secretary.

Stormy Weather

As I was saying, the girl of Hector's dreams turned into a nightmare after a few short years of marriage. For one thing, she got fat and kind of frumpy-looking.[13] Worse yet, she became hysterically suspicious. She used to go through Hector's pockets at night looking for incriminating evidence and she would piece together fragments of letters from his wastebasket to see what they said. She even studied his newspaper articles to search for coded messages. Once, when Berlioz received an invitation to go on a conducting tour, Harriet got so jealous that she absolutely refused to allow him to go off by himself. So he didn't go off by himself. Off he went with a soprano named Marie. Later, Berlioz moved into Marie's apartment so that Harriet always would know where to find him.

Out of the Frying Pan

Not that things were so great with Marie. She fancied herself a great singer, and insisted at performing at all of Berlioz' concerts. Actually, she was awful, but Hector couldn't figure out a way of breaking the news to her without getting her hopping mad. Occasionally he'd skip out of the hotel early, hoping she'd oversleep and miss the bus or something, but when he got to the next concert, there she'd be, big as life and twice as flat.[14]

[13]If you don't know what a frump looks like, any picture of Mrs. Berlioz will show you.

[14]Hector used to tell the story of a neighborhood woman who, on her way to work, passed beneath their window and heard Marie practicing. In the afternoon when she went home, Marie was at it again, "My God," the woman cried, crossing herself, "it's three o'clock, and the baby still isn't born yet!"

Decisions

Strangely enough, Berlioz' domestic life was deteriorating badly, so he made up his mind to stay away from women for a while and really concentrate on operas. It wasn't easy. "My teeth began to chatter," he said, "my legs started to shake, my nose bled, I was wild and dishevelled, in a daze, struck dumb." That was when he was concentrating on opera. Heaven knows what would have happened if he had stayed away from women.

Distractions

At any rate, here is Berlioz trying to forget women and remember operas, and not doing too well in either department. While he was trying to decide what to write his next opera about, for instance, he met this pretty Russian corset-maker, and he didn't work for weeks (on the opera). He sang bits of *Romeo and Juliet* for her and it was all very romantic and lovely, until her fiancé came home. Afterwards, when Hector was getting himself reorganized, along came Amélie, whom he met in a cemetery, and there went the opera again. Finally, when things were getting really desperate, Berlioz found the inspiration he was seeking. It came from one of the most beautiful women in Europe, Her Serene Highness, the Princess Carolyn Sayn-Wittgenstein. Don't get any ideas, though. She was just a friend.[15]

The Princess

Carolyn used to live in Russia on a big estate with three thousand serfs, and she developed quite a few funny habits, like smoking cigars and sprawling on bearskin rugs. She also had a terrible fear of fresh air. She would seal up all her windows and make visitors wait in an anteroom for at least fifteen

[15]To Berlioz, anyway.

minutes until they were properly deventilated. One day, Franz Liszt came to Russia on a concert tour, and he found her such a fascinating change from the average run-of-the-mill princess that he moved with Carolyn to Weimar. There they made beautiful music together for many years and everybody was happy, except maybe Carolyn's husband, who was still back in Russia trying to keep those three thousand serfs busy.[16]

The Inspiration

Carolyn's brilliant idea was for somebody to write an opera about the Trojan War. Liszt didn't want any part of it, though. He kept looking at the Princess draped on one of her bearskin rugs, and all he could write were things like "The Song of Love" and "The Dream of Love" and "Love's Castle." So Carolyn started pestering Berlioz, and puffed cigar smoke at him until *he* agreed to compose it.

The Creation

Berlioz wrote his own libretto this time, basing it on the first, second, and fourth books of Virgil's *Aeneid,* with a little Shakespeare thrown in for good measure for measure. For many months, Berlioz worked in the heat of inspired passion, and when he cooled down again he realized that he had composed a five-act marathon that would have run longer than Wagner's *Götterdämmerung* if *Götterdämmerung* had been written yet. Obviously, nobody was going to put on a monster like that, so Berlioz divided it in halves.[17] The first part, called *The Capture of Troy,* never was staged during Berlioz' life-

[16]The Princess never composed any music herself, but she did write a book. It was in twenty-four volumes, and it was called *The Interior Causes of the Exterior Weakness of the Church.*

[17]Now he had two operas nobody wanted to produce.

time, but at long last, in the fall of 1863, an impresario named Carvalho agreed to première the rest of the opera, which he named *The Trojans at Carthage*. Well, it may have been only half an opera, but it was still twice too long. Every night, for ten nights, Carvalho cut another number. Then, when it was down to the right size at last, he withdrew it from the repertoire.

Finale

Berlioz was getting old and tired, but he had one more opera to write, and one more woman to love. The opera was Shakespeare again, and the woman was Estelle again. Remember Estelle? She had lost her pink boots, and she was seventy and a great-grandmother, but Hector tracked her down, wrote her passionate letters, and went to visit her at home. "I began to shake violently," he said, "my soul leapt out towards its idol, I could hardly breathe, I could not speak, I felt my heart turn to water, and a thrill shoot through every bone in my body."

That's when Estelle let him kiss her hand.

Coda

So that was Hector Berlioz. A romantic first, last, and always. "I saw Heaven open," he said, "a Heaven of pure delight, purer and a thousand times lovelier than the one that has so often been described. Two powers can uplift Man to the sublimest heights, and they need not be separated. They are the two wings of the soul." That's what Berlioz wrote about Music and Love. And this time, he really meant it.

GEORGES BIZET

Everybody knows that "Carmen" is one of the most glorious operas ever written. Nobody knew it while Bizet was around to enjoy it, but as soon as he died, they knew it right away. That's the way things always happened with him.

Misfortune Cookies

Bizet was the original hard-luck man. He was the kind of fellow who stayed up nights to finish an opera by the deadline, only to find out afterwards that the production had been postponed for a year. He wrote a symphony, and misplaced the manuscript before anybody could play it. He wrote a newspaper review of a Paris concert, and the conductor challenged him to a duel. He entered a composing contest with only one other entrant, and ended up with second prize. Once he went to visit his girl friend, and tapped on her window at the precise moment her mother was emptying a chamberpot from the room directly above his head.

Nominal Difficulties

Everything went all right for Bizet until the day he was born, October 25th, 1838. His parents had him christened Alexandre César Léopold and the poor kid hated all three names. As soon as he could talk, he said let Georges do it.[1] Georges developed a great passion for literature, but his father wanted him to become a musician,[2] so he hid all the good books and made the boy practice the piano all day. Aimée Marie Louise Léopoldine Josephine Delsarte even developed a technique for changing Georges' shirts while he was practicing, so he shouldn't lose valuable time. Unfortunately, just when he was getting really interested, Georges was sent to his uncle François to take piano lessons. That character could have talked Mozart out of liking music. He absolutely detested all keyboard composers except Chopin, and he chopped the pedals off every piano in the house to tell more easily when his students made mistakes.[3]

Tonal Troubles

After years of lessons from Uncle François, Bizet learned enough to vow never to give a piano recital as long as he lived. Instead, he became a composer, but nothing went right for him then either. He wrote nine cantatas and nobody would publish them. He wrote dozens of songs and nobody would sing them. He wrote forty piano pieces and even *he* wouldn't play them.[4] In the stagework department, Bizet started working

[1]His mother, Aimée Marie Louise Léopoldine Josephine Delsarte Bizet, could never understand why anybody would want to struggle through life with only one measly name.

[2]That's a switch. See Handel, Berlioz, Strauss, etc.

[3]Uncle François may have inherited a number of habits from *his* teacher, who used to pace up and down with a heavy load of opera books balanced on his head, hoping that some of the musical genius would seep down into his brain.

[4]The first known performances of any of Bizet's piano pieces came in 1938, during a celebration of the composer's one hundredth birthday. With all the hoopla, somebody miscalculated, and the program went on two days late. One might have known.

on about thirty operas, but he only completed seven of them. After he polished them off, so did the critics. "His music sounds like the chromatic meowing of an amorous cat," said one reviewer.[5]

The Mighty One

In the case of *Carmen,* you'd imagine that everybody concerned would have realized that they were dealing with a masterpiece. With Bizet's luck, it worked just the other way. First of all, the story had to be completely redone, because in the original version by Prosper Mérimée, Don José is really Lizzarrabengoa of Elizondo, and Escamillo, the toreador, is really a picador named Lucas, and Carmen is really carrying on with Garcia the One-Eyed, and there isn't a single girl named Micaëla in there at all.[6]

Compositional Hazards

When the plot finally was straightened out, Bizet heaved a sigh of relief and turned to the music. Don't ask. To begin with, he had to compose the whole opera in his madhouse of an apartment, with his baby screaming, balloons popping, and the man upstairs giving piano lessons all day long. Bizet would wrap a big scarf around his head to shut out the clatter, but students would come by asking for advice, and publishers would pester him for pieces he hadn't quite gotten around to composing yet. Also clomping around the place was the maid's eleven-year-old son.[7]

[5]The others were even more complimentary.

[6]Mérimée claimed that Carmen was a real person, and that he got the whole story from Don Cipriano Palafox y Portocarrera of Tebla, who actually knew her.

[7]Nobody ever knew for sure who the father was. It could possibly be a coincidence that Bizet had come home for a visit exactly nine months before the kid was born.

Advance Warning

Long before the score was finished, the Directors of the Opera House decided to take a look at it. They nearly had a fit. For one thing, their theatre was a favorite spot for marriage brokers, for here their prospective clients were introduced to each other, and a sexy seductress like Carmen could ruin the wedding business for months to come. They were even more upset at the idea of having an unhappy ending, and they were positively hysterical when they realized that there would actually be a murder on stage. Bizet patiently explained that it was just a teeny little murder, and he promised to sneak it in next to a ballet and a parade and stuff so that nobody would notice. He also agreed to cut a few passionate scenes with Carmen's husband, who was a pickpocket in the original story,[8] but that's as far as he would go.

More Storm Signals

The next problem was finding a singer to create the title role. The first candidate mentioned in the newspapers was a café entertainer named Zulma Bouffar, but she considered it touffar beneath her dignity to be stabbed in the finale, and turned it down. Then the part was offered to an operetta star named Marie Roze, but she sank to the occasion and declined because the story was too immoral. That left Marie Célestine Laurence Galli-Marié, whose dignity and morals were more flexible. Bizet played his music for her, got her home address, just in case, and told the Director of the Opera that he had found his Carmen at last.

Monkey Business

He had. But from now on the Director haggled endlessly

[8]In fact, he threw the whole pocket-picking husband right out of the opera.

with Galli-Marié over salary and vacations, until she wrote a sarcastic letter to a friend, referring to the Director as a monkey. That wouldn't have been so bad had she not mailed it to the Opera House by mistake, and guess who was opening the letters that day? For months, Bizet was exasperated, convinced that the whole project was collapsing. It wasn't, though, and in the fall of 1874, Galli-Marié arrived in Paris to begin preparations for the première of *Carmen*.[9]

Tempers and Tantrums

What happened before was just fun and games compared to the chaos of the rehearsals. Before Bizet could count to anything, everybody tried to get into the first act. The men in the orchestra complained that their parts were unplayable, and the chorus threatened to go on strike because Bizet wanted them to move around in the crowd scenes, instead of just standing there staring at the conductor. Later, the women in the chorus made Bizet rewrite one of the big ensemble numbers because it was too difficult. And, since the librettists usually had better things to do than attending rehearsals with everybody screaming at everybody else, the composer even had to rewrite some of the lyrics.

Star Dust

As the battles with the chorus simmered down, Galli-Marié decided that she didn't like her entrance number, and she made Bizet rework it at least a dozen times. When she announced that she didn't care much for version #13 either, Bizet got disgusted, went to the library, dragged out a book of Spanish folk songs, swiped one of the tunes, and wrote "Habanera" across the top in big letters. Well, no sooner was

[9]She brought her pet monkey to show the Director that it was all a big joke. He still wasn't laughing.

Carmen settled than out ran Escamillo, yelling that he didn't like his entrance number either. This time Bizet was ready. He went to the library and dragged out the book of Spanish folk songs right away. But he couldn't find any more good ones, so he plunked himself down at a table and dashed off the "Tore-ador Song." "If they want garbage, they'll get garbage," he grumbled, which just shows you how little Bizet knew about writing popular operas.[10]

The Big Moment

At last everything was ready. The principals were set, the chorus calm, and the première scheduled for March 3rd, 1875. Bizet was quite optimistic, although by this time he really ought to have known better. Sure enough, the audience was so shocked at the opera that they didn't boo and hiss until way into the third act. One difficulty was that the performance took place at the Opéra-Comique, and it wasn't the least bit funny. On top of that, the performance itself wasn't so hot. The tym-panist miscounted his rests and uncorked a fierce drum roll right in the middle of a delicate aria, Galli-Marié lost her castanets and had to break a dish on stage to get something to clack, and the tenor who played Don José managed to go two tones flat in one number.[11] Worst of all, the Parisians were looking forward to a nice, lavish ballet, and all they got was a couple of scraggly-looking gypsy girls.

Conclusion

And so, *Carmen* had an unhappy ending in more ways

[10]He didn't actually use the word "garbage," but I'd just as soon not go into the matter any further, if you don't mind.

[11]To keep the tenor reasonably on pitch in future performances, Bizet rigged up a portable organ backstage, and had a student bang out the melody along with him.

than one. Only two or three of Bizet's friends were good enough liars to pretend that the opera had been a success. The rest slunk quietly away, and the composer wandered the streets half the night in deep despair. After a while, he began to feel a little better. Then the reviews came out. "Bizet's music is painful, noisy, blatant and eminently repulsive," said one of the kindlier critics. "If the devil were to write an opera," said another, " it would probably come out sounding very much like *Carmen*." Bizet's masterpiece struggled along for another several months, but the theatre was half empty, and the receipts from ticket sales did not even cover production costs.

Curtain

Exactly three months after the opening, Galli-Marié was singing the role again, when she felt a sudden chill during the scene where Carmen sees death in the cards. She managed to complete her part, then rushed offstage and fainted in the wings. Later, the word came. That night, at almost the same moment that the curtain had fallen at the Opéra-Comique, Georges Bizet, disillusioned and sick, had died in his country home outside Paris. He was thirty-seven years old. At his funeral, the orchestra played two of his overtures, and singers presented arias from three of his operas, and the organist improvised a grand fantasy on themes from *Carmen*. It was the first time in history that anybody had ever put on an all-Bizet concert. Just his luck he had to miss it.

Renaissance

Today, naturally, we know that Bizet's critics were wrong. Even they came to know it because, within a very few years, *Carmen* became the most fantastic success in the annals of opera. It was staged in Brazil and Latvia and Australia and

Norway and America. Brahms went to see it twenty times.[12]
It was given in Japanese and Estonian and Danish and Swedish
and Hebrew and Slovenian and Chinese and Portuguese and
Bulgarian. In Russia, it was a tremendous hit as *Carmencita
and the Soldier*[13] and in Spain they presented *Carmen* in a bull
ring. Yes they did. They hired a real toreador and a real bull
and they had a real bullfight in the middle of the opera.

Carmen Market

As the years went by, *Carmen* became more and more
popular. It was staged well over three thousand times at the
Opéra-Comique alone, and when the lofty Paris Opéra decided
to give it a brand new production, they fixed it up with horses,
dogs, donkeys, monkeys and (in the audience) General de
Gaulle. We've had movie Carmens and jazz Carmens and rock
Carmens and ballet Carmens. There was a Carmen at the Metropolitan Opera House starring Beatrice Lillie in kilts.[14] A
Russian composer has done a version using forty-seven per-
cussion instruments, and an American concocted one for solo
kazoo and symphony orchestra. We've seen *Carmen Jones* with
an all-black cast and *The Naked Carmen* with, never mind.
You know something? Maybe Georges Bizet wasn't so unlucky
after all. The only version of *Carmen* he ever knew was the
original, the one that has come to be called "The Queen of
Operas."

[12]Count Bismarck, who was usually much too busy breaking treaties
and declaring wars and doing other statesmanlike things to worry
about operas, caught the show twenty-seven times.

[13]For some reason it took three singers to do the one part of Micaëla.
Oh well, it's their problem.

[14]It was advertised for a run of one consecutive performance, a benefit
at that.

Giuseppe Verdi

Giuseppe Verdi was born in Le Roncole, a little Italian village not far from Parma.[1] Even after he became rich and famous, Verdi always stayed a small-town boy at heart. That's because he grew up in the town of Busseto, and you can't get much smaller than that.[2]

The Simple Life

For years and years, people fussed over Verdi, and he couldn't stand it. They tried to put plaques on his door and make him serve on government commissions and name conservatories after him, until he was ready to scream. All he wanted was to stay down on the farm and grow beets, but something else always came up.[3] He was hardly born when people started fussing with his name. His father called him Giuseppe, which was fine since that was the old man's middle name, and he wasn't using it much himself. But on October 11th, 1813, the one-day-old baby was registered with the church as Joseph Fortuninus Franciscus, probably because the priest thought that Giuseppe didn't sound sacred enough. Then, on October 12th, 1813, the two-day-old baby was regis-

[1]Unless you go in the opposite direction, in which case it's not far from Cremona.

[2]Unless you move to Sant' Agata, which Verdi *did,* later.

[3]Not necessarily where he'd planted the beets.

tered with the town as Joseph Fortunin François, probably because the clerk on duty was a Frenchman. As it turned out, Verdi's father could speak neither Latin nor French, so he just kept calling the boy Giuseppe as if nothing had happened.[4]

Musical Beginnings

When Giuseppe was eight years old, his parents gave him a harpsichord for a present. It was only a small, battered, old thing with broken strings, but the boy would fool with it for hours at a time.[5] One day, Giuseppe was fooling around with it as usual when, purely by accident, his fingers hit a C-major chord. He was thrilled, yet he wasn't able to recapture that interesting sound. All afternoon he tried to find it again, getting madder and madder when he couldn't, until he grabbed a hammer and banged the harpsichord even more battered and broken. As he grew older, Verdi took up the flute, clarinet and horn, but he couldn't figure out a way of playing C-major chords on those instruments either. Maybe that's why he decided to become a composer.

Operatic Beginnings

The first orchestral piece Verdi wrote was an overture to *The Barber of Seville,* and was he ever annoyed when somebody told him that Rossini had already done that. Next, Verdi went to Milan, and spent a whole year listening to as many operas as he could, just so it shouldn't happen again.[6] His first

[4]Verdi's father never was good at thinking up clever names. A few years later he had a daughter, and he called her Giuseppa.

[5]You can still see that very instrument today, in the famous museum at La Scala. Just look for a small, battered, old thing with broken strings.

[6]When the year was up, he went back to his desk and wrote two arias for *Faust,* an opera Gounod was going to compose later.

original opera was called *Oberto,* and when you read the libretto, you'll know why nobody ever had used it before. Still, Giuseppe was so proud of it that he would walk around the house humming the quartet.[7] *Oberto* was performed fourteen times in 1839, and just when the customers in Milan were beginning to complain about seeing the same show over and over again, bids came in to have it produced at opera houses in three other cities.

Fast Finish

Verdi was on his way. Or at least that's what it looked like until he came through with Opera #2, a bomb called *King for a Day.* Now we all know that opera plots are supposed to be silly, but this one carried the rule to ridiculous extremes. It's about Giulietta di Kelbar who is engaged to Tesoriere La Rocca except that she really loves Edoardo who is the nephew of the Treasurer of the States of Brittany who is a friend of the Marchesa del Poggio who is engaged to Count Ivrea except that she really loves the Cavaliere di Belfiore who is masquerading for a day as Stanislaus, King of Poland, so that the real Stanislaus can win over the Polish Diet in order to remain King of Poland at least until the end of the opera.[8] The audience didn't understand what was going on either, and they hooted and hissed so loudly at the première that the opera was withdrawn and never performed again.[9]

[7]It's not easy to hum a quartet. In fact, it's four times harder than humming the melody.

[8]Depending on how you pronounce "Polish," the Polish Diet was a lot like the Diet of Worms, only shinier.

[9]Well, yes, it *was* performed again, in 1951, but by then Verdi was a hundred and thirty-eight and couldn't have cared less.

Intermission

Verdi was crushed. In fact, he was so insulted that he tore up his contracts and announced that he would never compose again. Merelli, the impresario at La Scala, begged him to change his mind, but Verdi stomped off, and for nearly a year he did not write a single note. Then Verdi bumped into Merelli on the street. The impresario was all upset because he had a fantastically great libretto, full of madness and murder and all sorts of other lovely things, and nobody to compose the music for it. "Here, read it," Merelli said, stuffing the pages into Verdi's pocket and running off before the composer could stop him.

Temptation

When Verdi got home, he threw the libretto onto the table and tried to ignore it. But soon curiosity got the better of him, and he snuck a quick look at one of the verses to convince himself that he really wasn't interested. He read that page, and the next, and the next, then forced himself to close the book and go to bed. Naturally, he couldn't sleep. All night long, he kept getting up to look at the libretto again, and by morning he had the thing just about memorized. Still, he was determined to stick to his resolve. "Beautiful, eh?" exclaimed Merelli when Verdi returned the libretto to his office, "all right, then, set it to music." "Never!" Verdi screamed. "I want no part of it!" "Yes you do," Merelli shouted back, "now go and start composing it!" And with that, he shoved the composer out of the office and locked the door behind him. "What could I do?" whimpered Verdi years later, recalling the scene. "I returned home with the libretto in my pocket. One day I did a line, the next day another; now a note, now a phrase . . ." Within three months the entire opera was finished.

[100]

Comeback

The original title of the new opera was *Nebuchadnezzar*,[10] but when Verdi realized that *Nebuchadnezzar* is impossible to say, let alone sing, he retitled it *Nabucodonosor*. That didn't help a whole lot, as you can imagine (nothing rhymes with Nabucodonosor, except maybe now-a-word-from-our-composer—and even *that* doesn't work out right in Italian), so Verdi changed it again, to *Nabucco*. (Nabucco doesn't rhyme with anything either, but at least they don't spend half the opera trying.)[11]

Success

Nabucco became a fabulous hit. It was performed more than sixty times at La Scala in 1842, selling more tickets that year than there were inhabitants in all Milan.[12] Within months, Verdi was a national hero. He was applauded in the streets and serenaded on his balcony. Italians named sauces and hats and ties after him, and then they wondered why Verdi didn't seem more pleased about the whole thing. We know the answer. Verdi didn't care a fig for hats and ties and sauces.[13] All he wanted was to stay down on the farm and raise horses.

More Operas

For this, Verdi needed more money, so he started work on

[10]Don't laugh. There was a German opera about the same Babylonian king and that one was called *Die Gestuerzte und wieder erhoehte Nebuchadnezar*. Now you may laugh.

[11]The English were the only smart ones. They renamed the opera *Nino*, as in Casino, Pokerino and Philippino.

[12]This fact bothered musicologists, until a particularly clever one figured out that some people had gone twice.

[13]Especially Verdi Sauce, which is mayonnaise mixed with sour cream and spinach. Ugh.

his next opera, *I Lombardi,* which is about the First Crusade. Again it was a runaway hit, although it did mark the start of Verdi's endless battles with the authorities. Italy was then under Austrian rule, and the Austrians tried to keep it that way by censoring anything that remotely encouraged Italian independence. Naturally, the police objected to *I Lombardi* because the opera showed people fighting for freedom. After some humiliating bouts with the censors, Verdi had a brainstorm. He dedicated the opera to the Duchess of Parma, and when the Duchess said that she liked it the way it was, everybody had to shut up.[14]

More Problems

Evidently, Verdi couldn't keep dedicating operas to Marie Louise indefinitely, and as soon as he stopped the authorities moved in again. Worse, they now had him pegged as a wise guy, and no matter what he did, they wanted him to do it differently. They made him cut lines, drop scenes, rename characters, move locales, change centuries. *Joan of Arc* became *Oriette of Lesbo* when the censors got through with it; *Moses* turned into *Pietro; Ernani* was converted into *The Pirates of Venice; Attila* appeared as *Gli Unni*. At one point, people got so upset at having operas switched around on them that they mounted a protest boycott of all the theatres. It continued until the authorities got frightened and issued a decree stating: "If anybody, by obstinacy, persists in not frequenting the theatre, such conduct will be regarded as the silent demonstration of a criminal disposition which merits to be sought out and punished." And so, people started going to the theatres again.

More Changes

The censors gave Verdi a doubly hard time with *Rigoletto.*

[14]Somebody ought to write an opera about the Duchess of Parma. Her name was Marie Louise, and she was Napoleon's wife, even though most of her children looked more like Count Neipperg. When the Count died and Napoleon was unavoidably detained at Elba, Marie Louise had so many men pay her condolence calls that her Chamberlain had to post a sentry at her bedroom door to control the traffic. Eventually he had to post a sentry to check the sentry because the fellow couldn't remember which side of the door he was supposed to guard. Marie Louise could also turn her ears inside out. A perfect opera heroine!

For months he argued bitterly, but in the end he had to agree to transform his French King into an Italian Duke, and also to tone down the seduction scene.[15] Since Verdi didn't want to take chances with the Duke's major aria, "La donna è mobile," he simply didn't show it to the censors. In fact, he didn't show it to the tenor until the day before the opening. That way there were no security leaks, and before the censors could move in, the aria was much too successful to be tampered with.

Revenge

Don't think the censors gave up. They followed the opera from city to city, and whenever it was produced they rushed in and demanded a whole new set of alterations. They even changed the title, again and again, to things like *Viscardello* and *Clara of Perth* and *Lionello*. Verdi, too disgusted to argue, eventually suggested that they print up some new billboards saying, *"Rigoletto:* poetry and music by — — — — ," with the censor's name inserted. Then he went back to the farm and dug some drainage canals.[16]

Ball Game

There was an even bigger commotion over *Ballo in Maschera*. It started when Verdi decided to write an opera, called *Gustave III,* about the assassination of an 18th-century Swedish king. The censors were horrified, because they didn't want

[15]Later, when nobody was looking, Verdi toned it back up again.

[16]The Austrian authorities weren't the only ones who tried to censor Verdi's operas. In New York, in 1855, legal action was brought to ban a production of *Rigoletto:* such a lewd and lascivious work that "by its singing, its business, and its plot, was then and there such an exhibition of opera as no respectable member of the fair sex could patronize without then and there sacrificing both taste and modesty."

anybody getting any bright ideas about assassinating kings, and they insisted that Verdi change the title of the opera to *The Vendetta in Domino* and make it about the murder of a 17th-century Pomeranian duke. Verdi grumbled and complained, but he rewrote the thing their way. As soon as he finished, the censors changed their minds. Now they demanded that the opera be called *Adelia degli Adimari* and be about a 14th-century Florentine gentleman who doesn't get assassinated at all. Verdi was furious. He ranted and raved, and when that didn't help, he cancelled the production. That made the impresario furious. So *he* ranted and raved, and when that didn't help he tried to have Verdi thrown in jail for breaking his contract. Verdi responded by suing the Opera House for defamation of libretto. Then he went back to the farm to feed the cattle.[17]

Happy Endings, Kind-of

Months went by. The cows got nice and fat, and Verdi put in a new crop of corn, and by the end of the summer he had simmered down so much that he was able to reach a compromise with the censors. Verdi got his assassination back, and his 18th century, but he agreed to call the opera *A Masked Ball,* and change the plot to make it about a governor of Boston. Of course, the settings didn't look terribly American, and the characters, who are named things like Riccardo, Renato, and Silvano, didn't sound terribly Bostonian. But the censors were happy, and the impresario was happy, and the public was happy. Even Verdi was happy, because as soon as the arguments were over he could go back to his farm and trim the magnolias.

[17]That's not just a figure of speech. Verdi had seventeen cows, six rams and four oxen, all of them hungry.

Self-protection

Some trouble about this farm business was now looming. The more Verdi puttered around with his radishes, the more some people assumed he was a country bumpkin and tried to take advantage of him. Maybe Verdi had a thing about driving his own plow and digging his own ditches, but he was no sucker. When *Luisa Miller* was being premièred, the impresario tried to gyp Verdi out of his advance pay until the composer publicly threatened to row out to a French warship anchored in the Bay of Naples and ask for musical asylum. When conductors tried to make cuts in his scores, Verdi would point to the small print of his publishing contracts, which imposed a fine of a thousand francs for each omission in the original music. And when his publisher tried to chisel a bit on his fees, Verdi sat down and went through every single account, going back twenty years. He wound up collecting more than fifty thousand lire in back commissions.

Prima Donna-itis

No amount of cleverness could keep Verdi from having fits about some of the performers he was stuck with. "How wonderful operas would be if only there were no singers," he said once, perhaps remembering Cruvelli, who messed up the première of his *Sicilian Vespers* by suddenly disappearing for weeks and weeks.[18] Or maybe Fasciotti, "who screamed in a way that would have rendered her invaluable, in pants, as a shepherd in the Pyrenees Mountains," or even Fancelli, who was positively scandalized when Verdi expected him "not only to read the music as written, but also to follow his tempo and dynamics and, worse yet, to memorize the words!" During the

[18]She was on her honeymoon, Cruvelli explained when she returned. Sure enough, a year later she got married.

rehearsals for *Macbeth*, the two lead performers tried to bluff through their parts until Verdi had them go over the same duet a total of one hundred and fifty times. Then, with the audience already seated in the theatre for the première, Verdi made them throw coats over their costumes, and run out to the lobby for run-through #151.[19]

Fiascos, Inc.

The most horrible disaster was reserved for the opening night of *La Traviata*. The part of the beautiful, consumptive courtesan was performed by Fanny Salvini-Donatelli, a soprano who was plump, ugly, and overflowing with good health. Every time she claimed to be wasting away, the audience howled with laughter. Her coughs were puny, but when she collapsed in the last act, she sent up such a cloud of dust that the other singers could hardly be seen. Meanwhile, the tenor went hoarse, the baritone was almost inaudible, and as one critic reported, "The première marked an epoch in the history of colossal fiascos."

Calamity, American Style

If Verdi thought the première of *La Traviata* spelled disaster, it's lucky he didn't manage to attend one of the first American performances of *Ernani,* in 1855. First of all, the tenor was so nervous about missing his cue that he came on stage way ahead of time and had to wait around, trembling, while the perspiration washed off his makeup and part of his false moustache. Meanwhile, the basso strode out for his first

[19]The funniest part of this incident is that the duet was such a hit that the singers had to encore it five times. By then they could have done it in their sleep, and that was even funnier, because the Sleepwalking Scene was next.

number and immediately tripped over his own sword, skidding along the floor smack into the terrified chorus. When he wobbled back on his feet, his spurs got entangled with the soprano's dress.[20] Thoroughly rattled, now, he plumped himself down on top of the prompter's box and stayed there till the end of the act, beating time with his foot, and counting the rests in a loud voice.

More to Come

By the last act, the tenor was in trouble again. He made a grand entrance from stage left, only to discover that the rest of the cast was looking for him to arrive on the right. Then he proceeded to pull his sword out for his big aria, and it stuck in the scabbard. Frantically he dashed around trying to wrench it free, and when he succeeded, he couldn't fit it back into the slot again. In desperation, he lunged for the exit, but reached the wrong one, and that door had been nailed shut. The last catastrophe awaited him in the finale, where Ernani has to commit suicide. This time he loosened the sword ahead of time, but did too good a job of it. When he drew it for the deadly deed, the blade went flying off into the wings, and he had to dispatch himself with the hilt. The curtain came down, but Ernani had fallen too far forward on the stage and was still in plain view. The audience roared, particularly when the dead body sat up, looked around in horror, and rushed off.

Modern Mayhem

What is it about Verdi operas? Even in more recent years, they seem to have invited disasters. In one performance of *Aida,* the strap broke on Robert Merrill's sandal. He deftly kicked it off into the orchestra pit, then launched into his big aria, only

[20]She was a corker, too. "Her voice," said the local critic, "produced a precisely similar effect upon the ear which a dull razor might produce on the skin."

to have some helpful musician find the shoe and heave it back at him on stage. Then there was the time Sir Thomas Beecham was rehearsing the Triumphal Scene from *Aida*. He made the chorus repeat one section over and over again, and still they couldn't get it right. Suddenly, one of the trained horses on stage forgot his training. Sir Thomas stopped the rehearsal, glowered at the offender, then said to the company: "Disgusting spectacle, but gad, what a critic!"[21] Another great singer to suffer from the Verdi hex was Beniamino Gigli. As Alvaro in *La Forza del Destino,* he was being taken off in a stretcher when one of the carriers stumbled. Gigli tumbled off onto the floor and had to climb back into the stretcher on his own, while the audience howled. Then, bending over to pick up his sword, Gigli felt his pants rip all the way up the back. Fortunately, the scene took place in a monastery, enabling him to finish the act wrapped in a monk's robe.

Finale

No matter how much of a celebrity he became and no matter how much fuss his operas produced, Verdi always preferred the simple life. Once, when a group of well-wishers came to see him, he hid in a toolshed. On another occasion, he spent a whole vacation with ninety-five barrel organs in his basement —he had rented every last one in town so that he wouldn't have to hear them endlessly grinding out his own arias.

Verdi refused to go to Egypt for the gala première of *Aida* even though he had a personal invitation from the Khedive,[22]

[21]In the original production of *Aida* they used elephants in the Triumphal Scene!

[22]This particular khedive had commissioned *Aida* in celebration of the opening of the Suez Canal, but by the time Verdi had finished the opera, the canal had been operating for two years. So had the Khedive, presumably. He attended the première with his wives and it took three loges to seat them all.

and he consistently turned down honors and titles and citations and commissions. If you ever wanted him, there he'd be, down on the farm, planting conifers and working on the flower beds. "Which of your works, Maestro," asked an interviewer, "do you consider your best?" "No question about that at all," Verdi assured him. "It's the rest home for aged musicians that I had built in Milan." And when a friend asked him why he didn't write his memoirs, Verdi just chuckled. "It is quite enough that the world has tolerated my music so long," he said after a pause. "Never shall I condemn it to read my prose." That was Giuseppe Verdi. You would have liked him.

RICHARD WAGNER

Richard Wagner wore pink underwear, climbed trees, and liked to stand on his head, but right side up he wrote some nice music.[1] Did you know that in Italian the word "opera" means "works"? Wagner did, and when you go to any of his operas, that's just what you get.

First Impressions

As a boy I heard most of them when my father, who was a member of the Royal Opera House Orchestra in Copenhagen, took me with him to the rehearsals. I would sit there for hours, listening to the arias, all of which were translated, probably because the singers couldn't pronounce all those complicated German words. They couldn't always pronounce them in Danish either, but at least it didn't take so long. I remember my first Wagner opera well. By the time Tannhäuser had reached the Venusberg, I had reached the streetcar on my way home. It had become quite clear to me what Rossini meant when he said that Wagner had some fine moments, but terrible quarter-hours.[2]

Modest Richard's Almanac

In any event, Wagner was one of the most remarkable

[1] If you like operas.

[2] Then again, you should have heard what Wagner said about Rossini!

[113]

composers of all time, even if he said so himself.[3] It took him long enough to get there, though. He abhorred practicing, and didn't write a single note until he was fifteen. As a musician, Wagner may have gotten off to a late start, but he made himself obnoxious from the very beginning. As a baby, he would wake up the household by screaming at the top of his lungs every night. As a child, he drove his teachers wild because he would never fulfill his assignments. As a teenager, he made a tremendous fuss whenever he heard violins playing in fifths, claiming they made him see ghosts. Richard made his theatrical debut at the age of five, sewn into a pair of tights and fitted out with huge silver wings, and it proved to be a milestone in his development. Never again did he in any way resemble an angel.

Educational Data

Wagner didn't mind school so long as he could attract attention and applause. He recited poems and acted in plays, and became the undisputed somersault champion. Whenever they tried to teach him anything, he played hooky.[4] He did, however, manage to learn a few things. He learned to stand on his head, and to hang by his feet from balcony railings, and he got so good at sliding down banisters that his mother made him do it at home, for guests. At the University of Leipzig, it was the same story. He majored in gambling, duelling, drinking, and making love.[5] When he learned that he was supposed to attend classes too, he quit.

[3]Which he did. Frequently.

[4]In 1829, when he was sixteen, his family received a note from school complaining that Richard hadn't shown up in six months.

[5]With no panty raids in those days, Wagner and his friends settled for storming the local brothel.

Dramatic Moves

All this time, Wagner had absolutely no intention of becoming a great composer. He wanted to be a great dramatist. He wrote one play called *Leubald* where forty-two characters get murdered in the first four acts, and was he insulted when the audience almost died laughing. Since music is not a laughing matter, Wagner realized that the way to have people take his plays seriously was to surround them with serious music. And since nobody was good enough to write music for his dramas, Wagner reluctantly decided that he'd have to break down and become a great composer himself.

Starting Gate

Aware that he didn't know too much about composing yet, he began studying orchestral scores. He arranged Beethoven's Ninth Symphony for piano, and he bought a book on instrumentation in case he ever had to put the symphony back together again, and then he decided that he was ready to write an original piece all by himself. It turned out to be a Concert Overture, and since Wagner had trouble telling the instruments apart in the scoring, he put all the string parts in red ink, the brasses in black, and the woodwinds in green. The Overture was premièred on Christmas Eve, 1830, but the conductor must have been color-blind, because it was a flop. In fact, the audience laughed so hard you would have thought they were back at his play. All of this brought Wagner to the conclusion that music without drama was almost as useless as drama without music, and from then on he composed nothing but operas.[6]

[6]Except for a symphony, half a dozen more concert overtures, a piano sonata, etc.

Off and Running

The very first opera Wagner attacked was called *The Wedding*. It's all about a fellow who climbs through a window, surprises a girl who's about to be married to his best friend, and makes love to her until she pushes him back out the window. Wagner didn't finish the opera but he did gain experience by climbing through the window of the fiancée of an oboe player. In his next opera, the heroine gets turned into stone and the hero into a fairy. That one was never produced during Wagner's lifetime, and probably just as well. Opera #3 was called *The Ban on Love,* and the original version started with the storming of a brothel.[7] It also opened and closed on the same night because the orchestra got lost, the singers weren't ready,[8] and the husband of the prima donna was so jealous of the tenor that he came up on stage and slugged him.

Downbeat

As his operas flopped, Wagner's financial situation deteriorated. He owed money to friends, relatives, and tradesmen all over Europe, and he was forever sneaking across borders or sailing away in the dark of night to avoid debtors' prison. Things got so bad at one point that Wagner had to take in lodgers and shine their boots, while he himself stayed home for weeks at a time because his shoes had no soles.

Upturn

Naturally, Wagner couldn't go on writing bad operas forever, and as they improved, things began looking up again. *Rienzi* was a big hit,[9] and even though *The Flying Dutchman*

[7]His days at the University hadn't been wasted after all.

[8]One got so rattled that he started singing arias from another opera.

[9]It lasted more than five hours, but who was in a hurry?

never got off the ground,[10] his next creation was one of his im-
mortal masterpieces, *Tannhäuser*.

The Venus Caper

Wagner spent two whole years composing *Tannhäuser*,
although he could have finished it sooner had he not stopped
in the middle to write a Funeral Cantata for Carl Maria von
Weber.[11] He also was slowed down by his habit of playing all
the new tunes for his dog, Peps, and waiting for the hound to

[10]It came from the memoirs of a character named Schnabelewopski.
Next question.

[11]Weber had died eighteen years earlier, but who was in a hurry?

bark approval.[12] Anyway, the full title of the opera is *Tannhäuser and the Song Contest at the Wartburg,* and Wagner based it on history and legend. The legend had grown up about a knightly minnesinger named Tannhäuser who sang his nightly minnies in the 13th century. He also spent one of his vacations in the mountains with Venus, the Goddess of Beauty, and he couldn't stop singing about it. The history part was the Song Contest, which actually was held at the Wartburg Castle.[13]

The Première

The first production of the opera was miserable. The scenery didn't arrive in time for the opening, and they had to use some old sets left over from Weber's *Oberon.*[14] Then the Venus started complaining because she couldn't wear a girdle under her sexy costume, and the Tannhäuser lost his voice.[15] Luckily, some important critics were in the house, and they wrote long articles complaining that the love scenes with Venus were disgraceful and immoral and ought to be banned. Business picked up at once, and the opera became successful enough for Wagner to begin thinking of a sequel. This turned out to be *Die Meistersinger,* and it's almost the same show except that it deals with mastersingers instead of minnesingers, and it takes place in Nuremberg instead of the Wartburg, and

[12]Wagner liked to have dogs around the house. In addition to Peps, there were Faf, Fips, and Frisch, plus Pohl and Putzi, Russ and Robber, and Dreck and Speck. He also had a parrot that yelled, "Come upstairs, Richard."

[13]In the first chapter, on Bach, you'll find some more information on the Wartburg. You'll also find another footnote somewhere telling you to return to *this* chapter.

[14]Weber wasn't using them any more. See Funeral Cantata.

[15]His name was Tichatschek, and apparently he hadn't learned the part too well either. He horrified Wagner by singing his most impassioned aria to the wrong soprano.

it happens in the sixteenth century instead of the thirteenth, and it's a comedy instead of a tragedy. You could tell it was a genuine Wagner opera, though, because it lasted five hours and the critics hated it.[16]

Creature Comforts

By now, Wagner no longer had any doubt that he was the most fantastic composer the world had ever known. Under the circumstances, he couldn't see any point in denying himself a few simple luxuries. "I cannot live like a dog," he wrote to Franz Liszt, "I must be soothed and flattered in my soul if I am to succeed at this horribly difficult task of creating a new world out of nothing." Well, I don't know about his soul, but Wagner did all right for his body. He imported lilac curtains and satin quilts and silk ribbons. He ordered huge quantities of exotic powders and delicate cold creams and perfumed bath salts.[17] He installed soft lights and hung brocaded tapestries and put up Chinese incense burners and kept his music scores in red velvet folders.[18] He filled his house with golden cherubim and ivory figurines and hand-decorated porcelains. After that, composing was a snap. Whenever Wagner would hit a snag while working on one of his operas, he'd just stroke the soft folds of a satin tablecloth until inspiration returned.[19]

[16] "Of all the clumsy, lumbering, boggling, baboon-blooded stuff I ever saw on a human stage," said one of them, "of all the affected, sapless, soul-less, beginningless, endless, topless, bottomless, topsy-turviest doggerel of sound I ever endured the deadliness of, that eternity of nothing was the deadliest."

[17] "The bathroom is just under the room where I compose," he explained, " and I like to savor a fragrant aroma issuing from it.'

[18] To match his pink satin knee breeches, his pink eiderdown-padded house robe and his pink slippers with the rose bouquets!

[19] It was better than Schiller, who couldn't get inspired unless he was sniffing rotten apples.

Satins and silks are all very nice, of course, but Wagner was better inspired by women. There was Jessie Laussot, who kept him cheerful while he worked on the poem for Siegfried's Death.[20] Later, there was Judith Mendès, who got him so excited that, at the age of fifty-nine, he climbed trees to impress her.[21] But most inspirational of all was the beautiful Mathilde Wesendonck.[22] Wagner wrote her a polka "to melt the ice," and a sonata to "warm things up" a little, and finally he used Mathilde as the model for the heroine of his most overheated opera, *Tristan and Isolde*. Wagner had been busy writing his Ring Cycle when he met Mathilde, but he became so infatuated with her that he dropped it in mid-act, and started on *Tristan*. He even moved into a summer cottage on Mathilde's estate so he wouldn't have to travel so far to get inspired. Then he set to work. On the opera, too.

By the Book

Wagner completed the libretto for *Tristan and Isolde* in four weeks, which isn't half bad, considering the interruptions.[23] The music took him two years, though, and by that time he and Mathilde were just good friends. Fortunately, Wagner had an excellent memory, so the love scenes were as torrid as ever. In fact, Wagner may have overdone them a little. The opera was supposed to be premièred in Vienna, but the company abandoned the project after fifty-seven rehearsals.

[20]He wanted to run away with her, but couldn't convince either his wife or her husband to go along with the idea.

[21]Please see previous footnote.

[22]Sorry, but please see previous footnote.

[23]When it was finished, he read it aloud to his wife, his mistress, his mistress' husband, his future mistress, and his future mistress' husband. They all said they liked it.

On the Double

For several years, Wagner tried desperately to arrange for another production, but nobody seemed the slightest bit interested until he showed the score to the famous conductor, Hans von Bülow. Von Bülow thought it was fabulous. In fact, he was almost as fascinated with Wagner's opera as Wagner was with von Bülow's wife, and in 1865 there was a twin debut: von Bülow had Wagner's *Tristan* première, and Mrs. von Bülow had Wagner's baby. Thoughtfully, she named her Isolde. As it turned out, von Bülow was so enchanted with the opera that he wasn't all that upset at the affair. "If it had been anybody else but Wagner," he said, however, "I would have shot him."

All in the Family

As you may know, Cosima von Bülow was the daughter of another great composer, Franz Liszt. Liszt didn't exactly approve of this baby business, but he didn't condemn his daughter either. After all, he was still a bachelor.[24] Later, Wagner ran off with Cosima, had two more children with her, and married her. In that order. While we're on the subject, you might be interested to know that Isolde's brother was born right in the middle of Wagner's *Siegfried*. The opera, that is. Naturally, Wagner had enough to worry about without having to think up names also, so he simply called the baby Siegfried. The way I look at it, the kid was pretty lucky. Another couple of years, and he would have been called Götterdämmerung.

[24]If you think Wagner's love life was too involved, wait till my next book when I'll tell you about Liszt. Liszt's list included Daniel Stern and George Sand (both of whom were women, he said), the actress Lola Montez, and even a Polish countess named Olga who tried to poison his soup when he jilted her.

The Plot Thickens

To get back to *Tristan and Isolde,* it's a plain everyday tale of jealousy, treachery, sorcery, passion, remorse, anguish, betrayal, death, murder, and love. Actually, it has everything in it but a Wedding March, and that's only because Wagner had just used up his best one for *Lohengrin.* Isolde is an Irish Princess who claims to hate Tristan except we know better, and Tristan is a Cornish Knight[25] who is taking her to England to marry King Mark to whom he claims to be terribly devoted. Except we know better about that, too. Since Isolde would rather die than marry Mark, she decides to share a Death Potion with Tristan and get the opera over with. Now it might have worked, and for once we might really have wound up with a Wagner special that doesn't last all night. But no. Isolde sends Brangäne to get the potion. Brangäne is Isolde's Lady-in-Waiting, and she's been waiting around during the whole opera, with hardly anything to do but bring the Death Potion, and she can't even do that right. She brings in a Love Potion instead. Next thing you know, Tristan and Isolde are embracing each other passionately, and another two hours are shot.

Act II

In the Second Act, Isolde has married King Mark anyway, but you couldn't tell it without a program. As soon as the King goes off hunting, Isolde signals Tristan, and there they are again, embracing each other passionately, and singing tender love duets at the top of their lungs. Alas. Of all days, the King picks that one to get home early, and he catches Tristan and Isolde smack in the middle of a leitmotif. Furiously jealous, because he doesn't have much to do in the opera either, he sends in one of his soldiers to cross swords with Tristan. Tristan

[25]There's more to being Cornish than chicken!

adores cross-sword puzzles, but this time he gets wounded immediately, because his mind is still back in the love duet.

Act III

In the last act, Tristan is on a cot, peacefully suffering, when he learns that Isolde is coming to visit him. Obviously he can't take that sort of news lying down, so he gets up and sings another love song. Unfortunately, the strain is too much for him, and just as Isolde enters, he dies of the sword wounds in her arms.[26] A couple of others enter and get killed too, and finally Isolde dies her famous Love Death. I guess it isn't a barrel of laughs. But it does contain some of the most radiant music in all opera, which is something.

Coda

What else would you like to know about Wagner? He wrote some family operas, like the one about Parsifal's son, Lohengrin, who runs out on his bride just because she asks his name at the end of their wedding ceremony. Then there are the four Ring operas, twelve hours, forty minutes, and ninety leitmotifs worth, only I don't have the strength to go into them right now. Wagner also wrote an article in which he intended to prove that Beethoven was a great composer because he had a thick skull, and he spread the word that the way to save the world was to eat vegetables. And he sent two hundred and fifty-eight letters, forty poems, and seventy telegrams to the King of Bavaria.[27]

The only other impressions I have of Wagner are my father's. As a very young musician, Father studied music in

[26]That is, he dies of *his* sword wounds in *her* arms . . . you know what I mean!

[27]Please don't get me started on the King of Bavaria. His favorite color was pink, also.

Germany and was playing violin in the Hamburg Opera Orchestra when the composer came there to conduct his *Tristan and Isolde*. What a horrible man Wagner was, Father told me. He bullied the musicians and cursed at them, and kept them rehearsing from 8:30 in the morning until six at night, with a full performance yet to come in the evening. You'd think, my father used to say, that there was enough suffering on stage (not to mention in the audience) to satisfy anyone, but Wagner seemed determined to add some members of the orchestra to the fatality count. Still, his purpose was to achieve certain effects from the players, so Father fiddled while Wagner burned, and you know something? Eventually, Wagner *did* get the effects he wanted, and they were unbelievably thrilling. Maybe that's what genius is all about.

opera à la russe

The Russians not only didn't invent opera, they practically dis-invented it. Not that they had anything special against opera, mind you. It's just that opera is a form of music, and music was something the peasants liked, and anything the peasants liked the Czars didn't, and when the Czars didn't like something, watch out.

Banned in Novgorod

For hundreds of years, Russian rulers considered all sec-ular music-making a highly suspicious activity. The early Czars were especially nervous about instrumental music, because you could never tell what kind of weapons musicians might be hiding in their instrument cases, but they had it in for the wandering minstrels, too.[1] The Czars forbade jugglers to jug-gle, and they passed laws against "pagans who do the devil's work and spread temptation among the faithful by playing cymbals and singing immodest songs," and they even banned chess, possibly because some players liked to whistle while waiting for the other fellow to move.

More Nyets

The rules about sacred music were even stricter. No in-

[1]Wandering minstrels in old Russia were called skomorokhi, and they used to wander with trained apes and tame bears and dancing goats.

struments of any sort were allowed in church, which is why the men in Russian choirs developed those deep, organ-like tones. Women weren't permitted to sing in church at all, which is why the men in Russian choirs developed those high, falsetto sounds. Then the Czars tried to figure out why nobody showed up for services.

Steppe Up

After they got church music messed up enough to suit them, the Czars tried to ban all other types of music, especially if they were any fun. They forbade musical games, parties and dances, and they instructed the peasants to stop singing folk songs at once.[2] Even dancing bears were taboo, although the Czars could never find a way of explaining it to the bears. Meanwhile, if you were a troubadour in old Russia, you shouldn't have been. The Czars hated troubadours even more than dancing bears, because they could never be sure that they were singing the right sort of songs. The poor fellows were jeered at and stoned and hounded from village to village.[3]

Change of Grace

The first Czar to take an active interest in music was Ivan IV. In 1547, when he was seventeen, Ivan wrote a couple of church songs, and then spent most of the rest of his life building music schools so that people could learn how to sing them properly. It must have been about this time that the first Russian music critics were being heard from, because the Czar was soon known far and wide as Ivan the Terrible. Ivan actu-

[2]This may have been the first attempt in history to create a silent majority.

[3]Troubadours used to accompany themselves on things like gudoks, gusli, dumbras, and arfas, so maybe the Czars knew what they were doing.

ally tolerated other composers, so long as they were worse than he was. That wasn't easy. After a while, a lot of Russian musicians began to wish they had gone into some other line of work. One bushy-haired tune-smith was called Markel the Beardless after Ivan got through with him. Then there was the case of Stephen the Pauper. Don't even guess!

Import Quota

Gradually, other Czars started liking music, only by then they had chased away most of the decent Russian composers. In 1648, Czar Alexis solved that problem by inviting a whole bunch of foreign musicians to come play and sing for the Russians instead. Regrettably, he neglected to clear it with the Church ahead of time, and did Alexis ever hear it from the Archdeacon. An order immediately went out to cancel the concerts, confiscate the instruments, "and have all the jugglers whipped for plying their godless trade." In Moscow alone, the soldiers picked up five wagon-loads of instruments and burned them all in public bonfires. Here and there they considered using musicians for kindling, just to make sure they didn't try it again. But Alexis didn't cry over spilt musicians. He knew there were plenty more where they came from.

On to the Opera

It was Czar Alexis who ordered the very first opera performance in Russia. He did it to celebrate the birth of his son, Peter the Great. Peter wasn't so great then, but Alexis wasn't about to sit and wait until the kid grew up, so he built himself a theatre in his summer place, at Preobrazhenskoye—a cozy little place, with carved wooden candelabras, glittering raspberry-colored wall cloths, and gold-dust sprinkled on the costumes. There he got a company of German actors and singers to put on a cheerful opera for Peter's birthday party. The opera was called *The Acts of Artaxerxes,* and since nobody could understand a word of it, it was a tremendous success. Well, maybe it wasn't such a tremendous success, but Alexis loved it, and that's what counted. He stayed in the theatre for ten hours straight, and after leaving, made all his government officials go back with him to see the second show. Alexis then commissioned the same German troupe to produce another opera, called *How Judith Cut Off the Head of Holofernes,* and that one was even more successful. Russians always did like comic endings.

More Royalties

After listening to all those operas as a boy, Peter the Great grew up without any interest in music whatsoever. Fortunately, other things kept him occupied. He invented new calendars and devised new taxes, and he organized fire departments and prepared disastrous expeditions against Turkey and Sweden. When Peter had some free time he would drink himself into a stupor, or hammer nails into pieces of wood.[4] Every so often, he would personally cut the beards off his principal nobles to show them who was boss. Peter's daughter, the Empress Elizabeth, was much fonder of music, and she followed her grandfather's policy of importing foreigners to make it for her.[5] So did Catherine the Great, who took over in 1762. Catherine was crazy about operas, and the first thing she did when she became Empress was to commission one in her own honor. It

[4]Once, when the Czar business was slow, he slipped out of town and took a job as a ship's carpenter in Holland.

[5]Elizabeth flipped over French-style costume balls, especially the sort where men dressed as women and the women pretended to be men. She liked to go as a Dutch sailor.

was called *Minerva's Triumph,* and the performance was given on huge chariots pulled by two dozen oxen, and it lasted two weeks. After that, Catherine sent to Italy for Galuppi and Paisiello and Sarti and Cimarosa and any other composers they happened to have in stock, and she got every last one of them to write operas for her. Sometimes she did the librettos herself, to save time.[6]

Home-grown Opera

The Czars and Empresses might have gone on importing foreign composers indefinitely, but then one day along came Michael Ivanovich Glinka. Glinka was born at Novospasskoe in 1804, and is often referred to as the Father of Russian Music, which is not strictly true. It's just that he was the first Russian to think of writing something besides religious chants and songs about the Volga Boatmen.[7]

Educational Music

Glinka composed his first piece, a harp solo, at the age of fourteen when he fell in love, with a girl who played the harp, of course. He knew nothing about the harp and even less about composing, so it didn't work. Still, it was useful, because Glinka immediately started taking music lessons in case the situation should ever repeat itself. His next important music came four or five years later, just after he had become involved in a student protest against the cruel and tyrannical Czar

[6]One of her operas was called *The Early Reign of Oleg, the Varangian,* and then she wrote *Buslaevich, the Novgorodian Hero.* They didn't call Catherine "The Great" for nothing.

[7]Actually there were a couple of earlier Russian composers who wrote operas too, but who really wants to hear about Evstignei Ipatovich Fomin and *The Miller, the Witch Doctor, the Cheater, and the Matchmaker?*

Nicholas I. The uprising was suppressed and Glinka, who had a thing about not going to Siberia, rushed home and composed a big cantata in honor of the Czar's coronation.[8]

More Inspirations

So far, Glinka's career hadn't been terribly promising, but whenever anybody suggested that he forget about music and do some work or something, he broke out with all kinds of symptoms. It was even worse when he got a job in the Ministry of Ways and Communication. He complained of headaches and insomnia and indigestion and everything else he could think of, until his parents had to send him off to Italy for a rest cure. The cure consisted mainly of wine, women, and song, although Glinka didn't fuss too much with the song part. All right, maybe it wasn't restful. But it cured his insomnia like magic, and Glinka, as most tourists do, stayed in Italy until his money ran out.

Home Again

Along with his Italian cures Glinka enjoyed a lot of Italian operas, and they gave him a bright idea. As soon as he got back to Russia he vowed to write a Russian opera, earn enough money, and go right back to Italy. Well, he tried and tried, but there was a pretty young girl next door, and he just couldn't concentrate.[9] He realized that there was only one thing to do, and he did it. Then he composed the opera on his honeymoon. The opera was called *Ivan Sussanin,* and it was about this peasant, and everything was going fine until one day at re-

[8]I forget the words exactly, but they went something like All Hail the Generous and Bountiful Czar Nicholas, and Don't Forget, I Had Nothing to Do with the Uprising.

[9]On the music.

hearsal there was Czar Nicholas scowling at Glinka, and wondering how come the first great opera ever written by a Russian composer was about this peasant. Luckily, Glinka was a fast thinka. *Ivan Sussanin* was only the subtitle, he explained. The opera was really called *A Life for the Czar* and it was dedicated to Czar Nicholas, and besides, if his Czarship would excuse him, he had to go home and finish that triumphal hymn to the Czar which would make a perfect ending in the middle of the opera. So, Nicholas was very pleased after all, and appeared opening night and applauded very loudly. And Glinka's opera was a big hit.

Not So Happy Ending

Glinka was riding high for a while, but then his troubles started again. His mother-in-law moved in with him, and talked so much that it took him six years to finish his next opera. This was his masterpiece, *Russlan and Ludmilla,* but since it didn't include a hymn to the Czar, Nicholas never showed up and the première was a big dud.[10] After the opera flopped, his marriage flopped, and there was nothing left for Glinka to do but take some more rest cures. He got cured in France and Spain,[11] and then he got pickled in Poland, where he settled down for a while with two rabbits, a few dozen pet birds, and Angelique. He never did write any more operas, though. Pity.

Onwards and Upwards

Lots of other Russian composers came along after Glinka, so nobody got too upset. There were Bakhmetev and Schere-

[10]The Grand Duke Mikhail Pavlovich used to discipline wayward officers by making them sit through *Russlan* from beginning to end.

[11]Their names were Nini and Lolo.

metev, Dranischnikoff and Tchesnekoff, Azantchevsky, Brussilovsky and Starokadowsky, and their names all became household words.[12] My own favorite Russian composer is Borodin, mainly because he had the shortest name. Except for Cui, who was just showing off.[13]

Here Comes the Professor

Alexander Porfirevich Borodin was a gentle, kindly man, a general in the Russian Army, a famous chemist,[14] and the original Absent-Minded Professor.[15] Borodin was so absent-minded that he once walked out of the house in full military dress, complete with medals and plumed helmet, in fact complete with everything except his pants. He'd forget to get haircuts until he had a long pigtail dangling down his back, and in the middle of playing something on the piano he'd suddenly jump up and rush over to the lab because he'd remember that something was boiling over. He also often forgot to finish his compositions, which is why his list of works includes an unfinished symphony, three incomplete operas, and some variations without a theme.

Other Half

In 1863, Borodin tried to bring some order into his life by marrying a girl named Ekaterina Protopopova. He might as well have stayed single. Ekaterina used to sleep days and roam

[12]In their own households, that is.

[13]Cui wrote an opera called *A Feast in Time of Plague*. Shows you what kind of guy *he* was.

[14]His thesis on "The Action of Ethyl Iodide on Hydrobenzamide and Amarine" is not to be missed.

[15]He taught at the Academy of Higher Women's Courses and loved every lecture of it.

about the apartment all night, stumbling over the furniture. She also had an annoying habit of using Borodin's manuscripts for odd jobs around the house, like covering jars of sour milk. Once she lined the cat-box with a couple of manuscript pages of his symphony. Ekaterina loved cats, by the way. She let them parade across the dinner table, sticking their noses into everybody's plates and jumping on their backs. The only thing she had more of than cats were relatives. Rimsky-Korsakov used to drop over now and then, and he was always amazed at the number of people swarming all over the place, "falling ill or even losing their minds." They slept on couches or on the floor, or in Borodin's bed if he didn't get into it fast enough himself. Borodin got so confused that he couldn't even keep his mealtimes straight. Sometimes he'd sit down and eat two dinners in a row. Other days he'd wind up with nothing but a couple of soft-boiled eggs.

Back to Work

The inspiration for his most famous opera, *Prince Igor,* came to Borodin in 1869, when somebody sent him a book about the Polovtsi. The Polovtsi, in case you don't know any, were fierce Tartar warriors in the 12th century, who kept riding down from Siberia and insulting the Russians. Soon the Russians sent Prince Igor out to conquer the Polovtsi once and for all.[16] Anyway, Borodin started composing *Prince Igor,* and right away his mind wandered. He lost track of the fact that he was supposed to be writing an opera and put some of its best themes into a symphony. A couple of years later he began the opera all over again, but it was still slow going. Every so often he'd compose a few arias for it, but then he'd have to rush off to fix a test tube or feed the cats or something, and the thing never seemed to get any more finished. All in all, it took Boro-

[16]In the opera Borodin let the Polovtsi conquer Prince Igor.

din eighteen years not to finish *Prince Igor*. Finally, Glazounov and Rimsky-Korsakov got together and completed it for him. They knew there was no point in waiting for Borodin to do it any more. He had died three years earlier.

More Operatics

Peter Ilyich Tchaikovsky wasn't absent-minded, but he had opera problems, too. He couldn't finish his first one, he gave up on his second after sketching a couple of duets,[17] he ripped up the score of his third, burned the fourth, and never got past an "Insect Chorus" in the fifth.[18] Once, as Tchaikovsky got on the podium to conduct some orchestral dances from Opera #3, he developed the hallucination that his head was falling off, and he actually held on to it with one hand through the whole concert.[19] Tchaikovsky spent four years working on his next opera, *The Opritchnik*,[20] and he was so nervous about the première that he made advance arrangements to leave Russia three days afterwards, to avoid facing his friends. Or the music. But for once he needn't have worried. The opera was a hit, the final chorus had to be encored, and the audience cheered wildly until the composer came onstage to take a bow.[21] With all his

[17]If he'd written any more, Moussorgsky would probably never have spoken to him again. Opera #2 was supposed to be called *Boris Godounov*.

[18]Tchaikovsky was getting a lot of advice from another Russian composer named Balakirev, which probably explains the Insects. Balakirev loved them. He used to catch mosquitoes in his room and gently toss them out the window, calling "Godspeed" after them as they flew away.

[19]It took ten years before he worked up enough courage to pick up a baton again.

[20]Opritchniki (which is what happens when you have more than one Opritchnik) were a kind of secret police invented by Ivan the Terrible.

[21]Cui said that the opera was "commonplace, shameless, trivial, tasteless and makes us feel sick." What did I tell you about that Cui?

famous symphonies, ballets, and concertos, in some ways Tchaikovsky loved operas best of all, and eventually he wrote ten more. His towering masterpiece was *Eugene Onegin,* and even though Tchaikovsky was always the most self-critical of composers, this time he knew the worth of his accomplishment. It was, he wrote to various members of his family, the most sincere, the deepest-felt, the best-written opera he had ever done. Audiences all around the world agreed, and for a change so did the critics.[22]

Liquid Assets

Modeste Moussorgsky was another marvelous composer, until he wrote a song called "You Drunken Sot" and started taking it literally. He diminished more fifths than any musician in Russia, and his nose got so red that he had to run around explaining to people that it was still frostbitten from his parade days in the army.[23] Pretty soon, Moussorgsky breezed way past Borodin and Tchaikovsky in the to-heck-with-it department, leaving bits and pieces of a dozen unfinished operas. Once a group of friends offered him eighty rubles a month if he would promise to finish his opera *The Fair at Sorochinsk,* and another group of friends offered him a hundred rubles a month if he would promise to finish his opera *Khovantschina.* Moussorgsky accepted both offers, but he could never make up his mind which one to start finishing first. Finally, he compromised. He left them both incomplete. Another famous Moussorgsky

[22]All except You-Know-Who. "It is full of whimpers and pitiful whining," wrote Cui, "ridiculous, stillborn and utterly incompetent."

[23]Moussorgsky did attend Cadet School when he was young, but he was the despair of the commanding general. He kept getting drunk on vodka, like a Russian peasant, instead of on champagne, like a Russian officer.

piece was *A Night on Bald Mountain.* He managed to not finish that one four times.[24]

Good Enough

Moussorgsky's greatest achievement was his opera *Boris Godounov,* and one of the remarkable things about it is that he really did finish it all by himself. It made him feel so good that two years later he finished it all over again.[25] The opera was based on true events in Russian history, and if you don't believe me, go to the library and ask for the 1607 edition of "The Reporte of a Bloudie and Terrible Massacre in the City of Mosco, with the Fearefull and Tragicall End of Demetrius, the Last Duke, Before him Raigning at this Present."[26] This eyewitness account told everything that the opera does, plus what happened later, namely that after Czar Boris died, Dimitri advanced with his Polish armies and murdered Boris' son, proclaiming himself Czar. Then Prince Shuisky came along and murdered Dimitri, proclaiming *himself* Czar.[27]

Not Good Enough

Moussorgsky couldn't fit all that into his opera, but he did

[24]The first time, it was supposed to go into an opera. The second, he started turning it into a piano fantasy, and the third time he tried to make a choral piece out of it. When he couldn't get it to work as an orchestral intermezzo either, Moussorgsky gave up and let Rimsky-Korsakov finish it for him.

[25]Rimsky-Korsakov couldn't believe it, so he finished it a third time, just to make sure.

[26]It was written by a Dutchman, so you'll have to pardon the spelling.

[27]A few weeks later, a rumor spread that a mysterious light was hovering over Dimitri's grave. So Shuisky ordered the body dug up, cremated, and the ashes made into a cannonball. Then he shot Dimitri back towards Poland. That's one way to stop a rumor.

include a mad scene and a clock scene and a coronation scene and (naturally) a drinking scene. Then he proudly submitted the score to the Music Committee that had to pass all productions at the Imperial Theatres. Since it was a fresh, exciting, bold, inventive, incisive, touching, colorful, intriguing, brilliant opera, it was rejected right away. Moussorgsky had to go home and rewrite it. He added a whole new act, switched some of the scenes around and worked in a beautiful new part for mezzo-soprano. That last idea was the smartest of all, because just as the Committee was about to turn thumbs down again, their star mezzo announced that if they didn't produce *Boris*, she wasn't going to sing another note the whole season. So they did, and she did, and at last this cornerstone of Russian opera took its honored place in the repertory.[28] *Boris Godounov* became even more honored when another of Russia's great composers, Rimsky-Korsakov, switched most of the scenes back again, and improved all the orchestrations. He said.

Of Korsakov

Speaking of Nikolai Rimsky-Korsakov, he not only found the time to finish everybody else's operas, he wrote fifteen of his own. Most of them are about golden roosters and witches in disguise and animals that change into people and other contemporary social problems. One of his fastest-moving operas is called *The Tale of the Czar Saltan, His Son, the Famous and Mighty Hero Prince Guidon Saltanovich, and the Beautiful Swan Princess.* Before you read through the title, the first act is half over. The fastest part of all comes in the third act. This is the famous "Flight of the Bumble Bee," and by the time the tenor clears his throat, we're into the next scene. Rimsky also

[28]Cui didn't like it. He said it was "choppy, loose, immature, indiscriminating, self-complacent, and hasty."

wrote an opera about Ivan the Terrible, but he called it *Pskovityanka* in case Ivan still had any relatives wandering around. As a matter of fact, the only time he got into trouble with the authorities was when he composed an opera about a doddering, bumbling old king, and it was banned because everybody figured it was really about Czar Nicholas II. It probably wasn't, though. I mean, it wasn't Rimsky's fault that Czar Nicholas II happened to be a doddering old bumbler.

Incidentally, Rimsky's family name used to be just plain Korsakov. His great-grandfather, the Admiral, changed it.[29] It seems that the Admiral had spent a lot of time in Rome, and didn't want people mixing him up with all the other stick-in-the-mud Korsakovs who hadn't travelled any place. So he added the Rimsky part, since "Rimsky," in Russian, means "Roman." In other words, the Roman Korsakov. Nikolai came off fairly well at that. His great-grandfather could have gone some place else to visit, and then he would have been born a Hong-Kongski-Korsakov, or a Copenhagski-Korsakov, or possibly even an Antwerpski-Korsakov.

Came the Revolution

Modern Russian composers never have to worry about Czars interfering with their music. Only Commissars. In the Soviet Union today, operas are not only supposed to have interesting stories and pretty tunes, but a Message. And it better be the Right Message, too.[30] It all started in the 1920's, when the commissars threw out the Director of the Moscow Conservatory and replaced him with a Party man named Pshibuyshevski. I know you won't believe a word of this, but so help me, the first thing Pshibuyshevski did was to change the

[29]Rimsky never got to be an admiral, but he was in the navy, too. His specialty was falling off the mizzenmast into the ocean.

[30]Or the Left one, actually.

[139]

name of the school because "Conservatory" was too close to "Conservative." "From now on," he announced to the staff, "you will discontinue the unbearable practice of teaching about composers who are foreign and hostile to our ideals." Then, to prove the point, he ordered all the pictures of Bach, Chopin, and Schumann taken down from the school walls.[31] Next Pshibuyshevski did away with all exams, and devised other ways to destroy "the useless system of musical education that arouses in the student the unhealthy desire to compete for personal advancement at the expense of the collective effort." After a few years, he had done away with the competitive spirit so well that Russia didn't have any winners at the 1932 Warsaw International Piano Competition. Since the commissars were already boasting about all the Russian winners they were going to have, that was it for Pshibuyshevski. He was arrested, and the pictures of Bach, Chopin, and Schumann went back up on the walls in the halls.

Commissariat

There was other Pshibuyshevskis, of course. The Director of the Central Music Department was a former secret policeman, who made visitors leave their passports at the door when they went in to see somebody. Managers of opera houses were appointed because of their experience managing breweries or rubber factories. In 1940 a law was passed making it mandatory for all workers to put in a full eight-hour day, and one manager refused to permit a performance of Tchaikovsky's *Eugene Onegin* because one of the characters in it gets killed in a duel at the end of the second act, and therefore would have

[31]He hated those three in particular because Bach was a churchman, Chopin played in aristocratic salons, and Schumann was "an antisocial ultra-individualist."

worked less than seven hours.[32] Another city official demanded that musicians, hired to entertain in the park, play their full eight hours without intermissions. "The Government knows best what is and what is not possible," he kept repeating.

Big Shots

Not even the most important composers in the Soviet Union were safe from the commissars. In 1948 Prokofiev, Shostakovich and Khatchaturian, among others, were told that they were writing the wrong sort of music. Their pieces, the decree said, "reek strongly of the odor of the modernistic, formalistic, neuro-pathological, bourgeois music of Europe and America which reflects the decay of culture." Errors must be liquidated, the commissars said, or you know who else was going to be.

Prime Example

Dimitri Shostakovich was in real trouble for a while. He wrote a ballet called *The Limpid Stream* and the commissars screamed that they could see right through it. His opera, *The Nose,* was running for a time, but then the commissars picked it apart.[33] Shostakovich's next opera was called *Lady Macbeth from Mzensk,* and it was banned in Smolensk, not to say Minsk, Pinsk, and Votkinsk. Still, he understood perfectly well the relationship between Commissar and Composer,[34] and so he gave up writing operas. Shostakovich now sticks to sonatas and symphonies and other less subversive combinations.

[32]He finally gave permission on the condition that the singer remained backstage in his heavy fur coat, beaver hat, and makeup, until the final curtain rang down.

[33]Or blew it, to use the vernacular.

[34]One of his compositions is called *The Ass and the Nightingale.*

Aram Khatchaturian was smart enough not to write any operas in the first place. He kept busy with pieces like *The Song of Stalin,* a couple of Red Army ballads, and a ballet about collective farms called *Happiness.* Soon he became one of the most honored composers in the Soviet Union. He won the Order of Lenin and the First Degree Stalin Prize. After that, he got the Second Degree Stalin Prize. For a while he thought they were going to give him the Third Degree also, and he almost ran away.[35] But Stalin died, and Aram didn't get any more prizes. Unfortunately, he also didn't write any operas. The closest Khatchaturian ever got to writing an opera was his ballet *Gayne,* and even I have to admit that isn't very close. Luckily, it has some very nice music. Especially the Sabre Dance, which is a dance danced by a group of Kurds. In Russia, these days, that's a compliment.

[35]That may be the origin of the expression, Chicken Khatchaturian.

Ballet at the Opera

Almost as soon as operas were invented, composers started putting ballets into them. That way people didn't have to sit through so much singing.

Progress

Ballet developed especially well in France, because Henry IV passed a law banning opera productions entirely unless they had dancing. His son, Louis XIII, went further and danced in opera ballets himself to make sure he wasn't missing anything. Once he even wrote a ballet, composing the steps and designing the costumes and all. It was called *The Hunting of the Blackbird*, and the King got the idea for it one day while he was hunting blackbirds. Such are the mysterious ways of inspiration.

The King's Ballet

The production began with an aria by a old man who represented Winter. He came out on stage and then he went away again, and in between he sang something about how nice it was that spring was coming and everybody could go and hunt blackbirds again and Hurray for the Great and Bountiful Louis XIII May He Rule Forever in Wisdom and Glory.[1] The ballet had a very large cast. To begin with, there

[1]Would it surprise you to learn that the King also wrote the lyrics?

were two cage-bearers, a couple of pages, the chief falconer, the assistant chief falconer, a bell-seller and the bell-seller's wife.[2]

Act Two

After them came four soldiers, somebody named Thomas the Butcher, a crossbow carrier, a few porters, three country nobles, a farmer and his wife, and finally King Louis again, changed now into the costume of another farmer to show that he was just plain folks. They all danced for an hour or so, until the first old man was rested enough to do another aria. This time he represented Spring, and he came out on stage and then he went away again, and in between he sang something about how nice it was that summer was coming and everybody could stop hunting those darn blackbirds and Hurray for the Great and Bountiful Louis XIII May He Rule Forever in Wisdom and Glory.

Two in Succession

After Louis XIII came Louis XIV, who flipped over ballets even more than his daddy. Generally, he liked them on a grander scale, preferably with elephants and camels and typhoons and flying dragons and other contraptions that helped take his mind off the music. Louis had an Italian adviser named Cardinal Mazarin, who did odd jobs around the palace,[3] but no matter how hard he tried, the Cardinal could never convince the King to like Italian operas. Mazarin spent huge sums of the King's money to import Italian operas and Italian opera singers, but the King was not amused. "I am

[2]Louis liked to take the part of the wife, dressed up in female costume, and ringing bells all over the place. Ding-Dong!

[3]Like running the country.

not amused," he said, just to clear up any doubts on the subject. He liked the costumes all right, but he complained that Italian operas were too noisy and had too many notes going on at the same time.

Another Dancer

Louis XIV didn't compose ballets the way his father did, but he danced in many of them. Usually he preferred the more stately dances, because his high heels slowed him down. The King would also wear pink tights and silk stockings and full-skirted coats and huge hats with ostrich plumes, and you hadn't better laugh, either. The guillotine wasn't invented yet, but Louis had other methods. The King's most famous role was in a ballet where he played the god of the sun, and everybody applauded so loudly that Louis was known as the Sun King ever after. Later, when he got married, he ordered a musical drama with so much dancing in it that it took more than six hours to perform.[4]

Royal Influence

One of the ladies who kept the King occupied when he wasn't dancing or getting married was his cousin, Anna Maria Louise d'Orleans, otherwise known as the Duchess of Montpensier, or sometimes Mademoiselle de Montpensier, or even La Grande Mademoiselle. This Mademoiselle from Orleans decided she could use some Italian lessons, so she sent one of her friends to Italy to find a teacher. Well, it was Carnival time in Florence, and the fellow was having such a ball that he forgot all about his mission until his last day in Italy. Not knowing what else to do, he dashed out into the street, cor-

[4]His bride was fat, funny-looking and had black teeth, so he wasn't in any particular rush.

ralled a teenager who was singing and dancing, and carted him back to Paris. As it turned out, he could have done worse.

New Music Man

The boy's name was Jean Baptiste Lully, and he not only sang and danced but played the fiddle. The first time he tried to fiddle around with the Mademoiselle, she banished him to the kitchen and made him wash dishes. Lully didn't discourage easily, however. He just waited, keeping busy by singing dirty songs to the kitchen staff, until Louis XIV came to visit. Then, out he popped with his dishtowel, singing and dancing like mad, and whistling a little tune from a new ballet he was writing. Louis thought Lully was the funniest character he had ever seen, and immediately appointed him to his court orchestra. Before anybody knew what had happened, Lully had taken charge of the orchestra, and then he started composing music for it. After that, the closest he ever again came to a kitchen sink was when he put everything else into his opera-ballets. Lully, by the way, was the first fellow to use female ballerinas, and the King was so delighted that he kept ordering more and more operas. One production that Lully worked out had forty-five numbers, and took thirteen hours to perform.

Going Up

As Louis XIV's favorite, Lully kept getting richer and more important all the time. It didn't hurt either that he was one of the few people who could make the King laugh. Any time Lully wanted a raise or a new title or something, he'd just trot over to the palace, clown around a bit, and there would be Louis, rolling on the floor in hysterics, ready to sign anything. Soon Lully became as much of a musical tyrant as Louis was a regular one. He'd break violins over his musi-

cians' heads if they didn't practice hard enough,[5] and he got the King to arrest his rivals, and he even managed to get laws passed saying that nobody but Lully would be allowed to produce operas in Paris.

Counterattack

Periodically, his enemies would try to get even with Lully. They'd write nasty articles about him, or they'd tattle to the King about his carryings on with all sorts of mistresses, or they would wonder out loud how come Lully and a certain swishy nobleman were walking around holding hands. They needn't have bothered, of course. Louis would call Lully in for a tongue-lashing, take one look at his face, and break up in convulsions of laughter until all was forgiven. So, Lully kept on writing nice short operas with nice long ballets in them, and finally people decided that his music was so pretty that there was no use getting all worked up just because he happened to be a sneaky, conniving rat.

Curtain

If you think Lully had a strange life, his death was even more remarkable. He used to conduct by stamping out the rhythms on the floor with a big, long staff, and one day he accidentally put his foot where the floor should have been, stamped on the foot, and got blood poisoning. Lully wasn't about to go without pulling one last stunt, however, and his final accomplishment was cheating heaven itself. He was getting weaker and weaker until a father confessor came to absolve the composer of his sins. The priest had heard all those stories about the mistresses and the broken violins, and he

[5]The players affectionately called him "le ladre," which means "the scurvy one."

made up his mind to get some sign of genuine repentance before he gave the absolution. After some preliminary haggling, the priest demanded that Lully destroy one of his operas that happened to be based on a particularly wicked story. Making a big show of remorse, Lully handed over the manuscript, which the priest promptly burned in the fireplace. He then gave the blessing and left. Hardly had the door closed behind him, when Lully called in his assistant, made him get out his spare copy of the opera, and before drawing his last breath, ordered another production put into rehearsal immediately.

Aftermath

After Lully, other opera composers came along in France, but they had all learned their lesson, and invariably included a ballet, usually at the beginning of the last act, so that the late-comers wouldn't miss it. The singing seemed to be getting worse and worse,[6] and the plots were getting sillier and sillier.[7] But the ballets got bigger and better until French composers finally realized they could write ballets without operas, and avoid trouble with the prima donnas.

Case en Point

One of the nicest opera-less French ballets was written in 1924 by Francis Poulenc. It is called *Les Biches*, which means

[6]"The actresses are almost in convulsions," wrote Jean-Jacques Rousseau, "forcing loud cries from their lungs, with their hands clenched against their breasts, their heads thrown back, their countenances inflamed, their veins swollen, their bodies heaving. It is difficult to know if the eye or the ear is the more disagreeably affected, because their efforts cause as much suffering to those who look at them, as their shrieking does to those who listen."

[7]"Opera," said Saint-Évremont, "is a bizarre mixture of poetry and music where the writer and the composer, equally embarrassed by each other, go to a lot of trouble to create an abomination."

approximately what you think it does, and for exactly that reason it was called *The House Party* when the ballet first appeared in America. Oddly enough, *Les Biches* actually *is* about a house party, so Poulenc didn't have to bother working out much of a plot. The various guests just spend the whole evening trying to make love to one another.

At Home in the House

As the curtain rises, we see an enormous room, with windows at the back, surrounded by painted blue curtains, and with a big green couch in the middle of the floor. Otherwise the stage is completely empty. Obviously this is too good to last, and soon twelve girls come in, all dressed in pink, so you can tell them from the window curtains. The girls dance around for a while, and go out the windows. Next some boys come in and dance around for a while, showing off in front of the girls, who had rushed back in as soon as they heard that there were boys there. After a couple of minutes, the boys stand on the green couch and lift the girls over it. Then the hostess comes in, dressed in yellow, so you can tell her from the couch. She is very sleepy, which is a little surprising, since she hasn't done anything yet. She orders the boys to clear the couch, and drapes herself across it to rest. Just then, enter two boys, more handsome than the others. The hostess decides that she isn't as sleepy as she thought, joins them and the rest of the party in a final fling, and the ballet ends in a burst of excitement.

Conclusion

So much for Ballets at the Opera. Until the next chapter, which is about More Ballets at the Opera.

More Ballets at the Opera

As you know from the previous chapter, Frenchmen really went for ballet in a big way. It got to the point where all choreographic terms (entrechat, pirouette, arabesque, and so on) invariably were given in French, no matter where in the world the ballet was being performed. One of the most famous French ballets takes place in Charles Gounod's opera *Faust*, which is about a fellow who sells his soul to the devil. Historically, Faust was a magician who lived in the 15th century. On his travels, he exhibited a trained dog and a trained horse, and everybody was so astonished at the tricks that they assumed his animals were devils in disguise. Pretty soon they started wondering about Faust, too. According to the encyclopedia, Faust's friends called him all sorts of pet names, like Drunken Fool and Vain Babbler, but never to his face, because they were afraid of being bewitched. Eventually Faust died, and everybody said, "Aha! the Devil got his soul at last!"

The Legend Lives On

Within a few years the story of the magician started cropping up in folk ballads, dramas, books, poems, and even puppet plays. Faust thing you know, musicians followed suit, and the story started cropping up in symphonies, waltzes, ballets, oratorios, and operas. One of those operas, as I've said, is Gounod's, and the Devil in it, called Mephistopheles, will go to great bother to service a potential customer. He absolutely guarantees Faust money, youth and power, and his soul back within thirty days if not delighted. He even throws in the beautiful Marguerite as an added attraction, on the sin-now-roast-later plan.

Dénouement

All this takes four acts, and at the end of them Faust still isn't sure that his soul is for sale. This meant that Gounod had to write a Fifth Act, and this time he didn't fool around. He put in this big, lavish, ballet sequence, during which Mephistopheles conjures up the spirits of all the sexiest women in history. Out comes Cleopatra on her barge of gold, and Helen of Troy, she of the face that launched a thousand ships. Faust doesn't care much for boats, though, so Mephistopheles calls up a whole bevy of Nubian slave girls. They all dance seductively around Faust and after fifteen minutes of that he's ready to agree to anything. So the deal is made, and it's a lucky thing, or the opera might have lasted until who-the-Mephisto-pheles-knows.

Czeching In

You don't have to be French to put ballets in your operas, and another fellow who had a devil of a good idea for a dance segment was the Czech composer Jaromir Weinberger. It was for his comic opera *Schwanda*, the full title of which is *Schwanda der Dudelsackpfeifer*, and you must admit that's pretty funny, considering that the opera hasn't even started yet. Dudelsackpfeifer means bagpipe player, and if you've ever heard a Czech peasant trying to play the bagpipes, you know the opera is getting funnier all the time. In any event, our hero,

Schwanda, is the best dudelsackpfeifer in all of Bohemia.[1] One day he pays a visit to Queen Iceheart, who warms up to him immediately. Soon he's playing her such a lively polka that her heart simply melts with joy.

Complications

Just then, Schwanda's wife comes in and sees the big puddle. She's terribly jealous, but Schwanda denies everything. "May the Devil take me on the spot if the Queen so much as kissed me," he says. So, the next scene takes place in Hell. It's a pretty hot scene too, with Schwanda winning his soul back from the Devil in a poker game, and setting all the little devils to furious dancing with a fiendish fugue. Today, when you hear the Polka and Fugue from *Schwanda*, it's almost always played by a dudelsackpfeiferless orchestra, which goes to show you what a sad state contemporary opera is in.[2]

Olé

Manuel de Falla, who was born in Spain in 1876, also wrote a lot of dance music, both in and out of operas. He was a fine pianist, but there's no profit in that, of course, so he decided to become a composer. *The Three-cornered Hat,* his most famous ballet, was written in 1919. The scene is a small Spanish village, and from behind the closed curtain come the sounds of heel-tapping, castanet-clacking, and frenzied shouts of Olé! Olé! Olé! When they finally get the curtain up, we see a miller standing in front of his house, trying to teach a black-

[1]At least, that's what it says in the program notes. Weinberger never lets him dudel one single sackpfeif in the whole opera.

[2]When the Metropolitan Opera first produced *Schwanda* on November 7th, 1931, they were afraid that nobody would be able to understand the Czechoslovakian words, so they had the whole thing translated. Into German. Well, it was a good try.

bird to whistle the time of day. Suddenly, his beautiful wife comes out of the house and teases the miller because his whistle is slow. He chases her around playfully, and, laughing merrily, they dance off into the house, which leaves the stage completely empty, so we have to start all over again.

The Villain

This time, in comes the proud and haughty Governor of the Province. You can tell right away he's the proud and haughty Governor of the Province because he's wearing the title of the ballet—his symbol of power and position being the three-cornered hat. He is, however, pretty stupid, even for the Governor of a Province. Besides, as soon as he sees the miller's beautiful wife, he forgets all about Governing the Province. Hiding in the bushes, he watches the girl dance a brilliant fandango, until he gets so excited that he dashes out of the bushes and fandangles some money in front of her. She only laughs, and leads the Governor on a wild chase around the house until he collapses from exhaustion.

If at First You Don't Succeed

Later that night, the Governor sends his Province Troopers over to arrest the miller and get him out of the way. Then, as soon as the villainous deed is done, the Governor sneaks back to the house and starts chasing the miller's beautiful wife all over again. Don't fret. She can take care of herself. She trips him up, pushes him into a pond, and shoots at him with buckshot. By now, even the Governor is starting to catch on to the fact that she doesn't care for him, so he hangs up his sombrero to dry and goes inside to take a nap. Meanwhile, the miller escapes from jail, steals the Governor's three-cornered hat, rejoins his beautiful wife, and they live

Happily Ever After. Not so the haughty Governor of the Province. He lives Terribly Ever After. His own soldiers can't recognize him without his three corners, and drag him, instead of the miller, back to jail!

One from the Trunk

The last dance music I ought to tell you about is a ballet for elephants, which at first glance are pretty silly animals to write a ballet for. Not that I have anything against the elephant. In fact I'm very fond of this clever and good-humored colossus. What's more, if there were no elephants, there would be no tusks and no ivory and we'd all be in trouble. Can you imagine playing chopsticks on the black keys only? No, I'm all for elephants.

Magnum Opus

And so, Igor Stravinsky wrote an Elephant Polka and brought a copy to the Metropolitan Opera. The Met wanted no part of it. They had enough trouble cleaning up after the horses in Wagner's *Die Walküre*. So Stravinsky took the polka to the Ringling Brothers' Circus. The Ringling Brothers at first were doubtful, too. They thought the tune was OK, but they didn't care for the choreography much. It just didn't ringle the bell. Fortunately, they called in George Balanchine, and before long he fixed up some much better steps for the elephants.

Basic Training

After that, the main problem was teaching the steps to the corps de ballet. Whoever started that rumor about elephants never forgetting should have been there. They were forgetting all over the place. Balanchine would explain a step to the elephants over and over again, and what happened? The next morning, all they could remember was how to walk around the ring chomping on each other's tails.[3] Finally, opening night arrived, and Balanchine was so nervous that he rushed out and hired a couple of ballerinas for safety's sake, just in case the elephants forgot their parts again. But they didn't. The Circus Polka was a hit, and it marked an important turning point in Stravinsky's career. It was the last time he ever wrote anything for elephants.[4]

[3] And that wasn't even part of the ballet.

[4] "I never saw the ballet myself," the composer said later, "but I met Bessie (the prima pachyderm) and shook her foot."

OPERETTAS:

Offenbach and Sousa

Operettas are just like operas, only not so much. Sometimes they are called light operas, because they're shorter and the prima donnas weigh less.

In the Beginning

The very first comic opera was composed in 1639 by two Italians named Mazzocchi and Marazzoli, which was enough to start anybody laughing. Giulio Rospigliosi, who wrote the libretto, was so ashamed of himself that he gave up the theatre and joined the church. Eventually, he became Pope Clement IX. How repentant can you get?

In the Middle

Some Italian composers were too busy writing serious operas to worry about funny ones. Marc'Antonio Cesti worked out *Il Pomo d'oro* in sixty-six scenes, with twenty-four different stage sets, and forty-eight solo roles, in addition to chorus and ballet. The only funny thing about the whole thing was the look on the producer's face when the bill came. But gradually the idea caught on, and pretty soon almost everybody was writing comic operas, including Pergolesi, who used to sneak his comedies in between the acts of church dramas, and

Leonardo Vinci, no relation to Da, who became a monk to get away from one of his mistresses.[1]

In the End

Comic operas soon became popular all over Europe, and many countries began developing their own distinctive style. In England, light operas were called masques, since the performers usually wore masks, and in France, comic operas were called Opéra-Comique, except that you couldn't count on it. For some reason, the French find talking within an opera terribly amusing, so anything with spoken passages is automatically called Opéra-Comique. Even tragedies. This can be quite annoying, since half the time you're not sure whether you're supposed to laugh or cry until it's too late.[2] In Germany, comic operas were called singspiels, because the actors sang a little and spieled the rest of the time. Also, I remember from my childhood in Copenhagen that my parents took me to hear syngespil, which are just like singspiels if you have a Danish accent.

Back to Paris

The beginnings of French operetta were not very promising, but things worked out, so don't worry. One of the first composers to experiment with it was Florimond Ronger, who, for reasons unknown, changed his name to Hervé.[3] Hervé used to work at an insane asylum in Paris, and many of his early works were written for the patients to perform. This didn't turn out nearly so badly as you might have expected,

[1]He didn't get far enough away, and she poisoned him.

[2]The way to tell is to look at the stage just before the curtain falls. If anybody's left standing, it was a comedy.

[3]Possibly to avoid being called The Lone Ronger.

since several of the inmates thought they were opera singers. Hervé's most famous operetta was called *The Mad Composer,* and now that you mention it, he *was* getting a trifle eccentric. Towards the end of his life, he made some money singing in Egypt and conducting in London,[4] neither of which helped the cause of French music much. In fact, the only reason I'm mentioning all this is that the light-hearted tunes and light-headed plots Hervé like to use were adopted and developed into a brilliant new national form by Jacques Offenbach, the man Rossini dubbed "the Mozart of the Champs Elysées."

Offenbach

Just to make it difficult, Jacques Offenbach wasn't born in France at all. He wouldn't even have been born an Offenbach, except that his father, Isaac Eberst, used to be a cantor in the little German town of Offenbach. When Isaac moved to Cologne, he wanted everybody to know where he came from, so he changed the family name to Offenbach. Considering that he might just as easily have come from the little German towns of Langenschwalbach, Pfaffenhofen or Brunsbuttelkoog, it wasn't such a bad deal.

First Flights

Although his father was dead set against his taking up an instrument, Jacques managed to wangle a cello out of some doting relatives, and took lessons without anybody finding out. His father finally got wind of it when the boy was ten, but by then Jacques had already learned how to slap the bottom of the cello to imitate a dog barking, and how to squeal his bow across the strings to mimic the trilling of a bird. Then his father gave in and let him take more lessons, and after

[4]Not simultaneously, of course!

many years of further study, Offenbach could also make his cello sound like geese hissing, ducks quacking, and women chattering.

Shaping Up

When he moved to Paris, Offenbach got a job in the cello section at the Opera House, but he didn't stay there long. After all, he had worked up this great waterfall imitation, and all the conductor wanted him to do was to play the dumb old music of the operas. As revenge, he used to skip every second note in the score, or else he would run a long cord from one music stand to another, which created weird vibrations whenever the cello section played in unison. Every time he was caught, his pay was docked, and when Offenbach began owing more in fines than his salary could cover, he quit.

The Virtuoso Life

It was all for the best. He became a soloist and toured all over Europe, and everybody thought he was fantastic. Felix Mendelssohn was his accompanist once, in London, and was left speechless by Offenbach's cello stunts.[5] Even when Offenbach retired from concertizing, the cello came in handy. Or at least the case, which he often used as a shopping bag when he went to the vegetable market.

New Career

Offenbach's next job was conducting at the Théâtre Français, but he didn't like that much better than playing in the orchestra. The more Offenbach conducted other people's operas, the more he knew he could write better ones himself,

[5]That must have been when Mendelssohn went home and wrote all those Songs Without Words.

although he didn't do so right away. He started with waltzes, and he was so proud when he sold a couple of them that he threw away all his shabby old clothes, and bought himself a nifty new outfit, complete with a high-buttoned jacket, velvet collar, and a pair of fancy patterned trousers. He let his side-burns grow and started wearing a monocle. Soon he became the smartest dresser in Paris, with one small exception. He kept forgetting to button up his pants. It got so bad that his wife developed a special code word to tell him that his fly was open. Whenever she started talking about "Monsieur Durand," Offenbach would excuse himself and go out to the kitchen for a glass of water or something.

[161]

Side Job

The waltzes sold so well that Offenbach's next assignment was to convert Meyerbeer's tragic opera *Les Huguenots* into waltz time.[6] Poor Meyerbeer. The original plans for this five-act opera called for a lavish garden with several bathing pools, a huge château banquet hall, a large meadow, a barricaded street, an elegant Parisian salon, and the River Seine with a sumptuously decorated barge on it—and now all that was left was a bunch of waltzes. (Wagner used to go to Meyerbeer's operas every so often, but wasn't terribly impressed. "He aimed for a mongrel, fickle, bigoted, frivolous, shameless hodgepodge," Wagner wrote, "but owing to the leathery texture of his musical mind, it never quite came off."[7])

More Composing

With all that experience behind him, Offenbach was ready for the big plunge. He bought out the lease of a broken-down old theatre on the Champs Elysées, completely reconditioned the place, and sat down to compose operettas for it. He wrote one called *The Divided Turnip,* another about *Lady Apple,* and a third, called *King Carrot,* which had a whole chorus of vegetables in it. The idea must have been that if the shows flopped, Offenbach could at least eat the props. Fortunately, none of the shows flopped. On the contrary, audiences flipped. Before long. Offenbach was turning out operettas at an unbelievable pace. He wrote eight of them in 1855, seven in each of the next two years, and thereafter he maintained an average of something like three or four entirely new productions per year, until his output reached the astonishing total of ninety-seven.

[6]He worked hard, too. The orgy scenes weren't all that difficult, but you try to pep up a massacre in three-quarter time, and you have problems.

[7]I forget what Wagner said about the waltzes.

Orpheus

Offenbach's most famous operetta was called *Orpheus in the Underworld* and it was based on the famous Greek legend. According to mythology, Orpheus was the son of Calliope and Apollo, and he was the best lyre player in Greece. Even his mother said so, and she had known some pretty fancy lyres in her time.

Lady in the Case

Orpheus had a wife named Eurydice, and one day she died of snake bite. That wasn't fair at all, since Eurydice had only bitten a tiny snake, so Orpheus took his lyre and went down to the Underworld, as Heck was called in those days. Furthermore, he went right up to Pluto, the King of the Underworld, and played the lyre for him. He played it louder and louder until Pluto told him all right take Eurydice back home. The only catch was that Orpheus was not allowed to look at her before they got back to earth. Everything went fine until Orpheus got one foot away from earth. Then curiosity got the better of him, and he looked back to see whether Eurydice was still there. Well, she was there then, but as soon as he looked around she wasn't there any more. Orpheus took the whole thing amazingly bravely. He picked up his lyre, went home, and began charming a pretty shepherdess named Chloe. (This must have made Daphnis pretty sore, but that's another operetta.)

This Operetta

Since Offenbach didn't understand Greek, he got the plot pretty well confused: Orpheus plays the fiddle, not the lyre, and pays more attention to a nymph named Maquilla than to mythology. For her part, Eurydice is madly in love with both Aristaneus, a honey-manufacturer who turns out to be Pluto

[163]

in disguise, and Jupiter, who turns himself into a buzzing fly so that he can get into her room through the keyhole. The plot gets more and more complicated, and it only reverts to the mythological version near the very end, when Orpheus heads for home. In the operetta, the thought of losing Eurydice so annoys Jupiter that he throws a thunderbolt at Orpheus. Orpheus turns around to say ouch, and as he does, Eurydice is gone forever. Still, there's a happy ending. Orpheus is happy because he can go back to his nymph, Eurydice is happy because she can flit back and forth between Pluto and Jupiter, and the audience is happy because it isn't past midnight for a change.

Production Problems

Just because the plot of *Orpheus in the Underworld* is complicated, don't think it was simple to put it on. The day of the première, a gas main burst, and they had to use candles instead of footlights. Then the soprano suddenly decided that her costume in the finale wasn't flattering enough, and Offenbach had to run all over Paris looking for a genuine tiger skin. Later, a rejected librettist showed up, trying to convince the composer to let him rewrite the plot, the piccolo player developed a fever blister and had to be replaced, the censor dropped by to wonder how come the fellow who played Jupiter looked so much like Napoleon III, and to top it all, a friend of Offenbach's rushed in to demand that the composer drop everything and act as his second in a duel. It was a miracle that everything did come together on schedule, and Offenbach himself conducted the première, on October 21st, 1858.

Double Take

Surprise! It wasn't a hit at all, and might have closed down had it not been for Jules Janin, the most influential critic in Paris. Janin wrote column after column denouncing *Orpheus* as immoral, indecent, scandalous, shocking, and "a profanation of holy and glorious antiquity." Naturally, the operetta at once became the toast of Paris. The audiences went especially wild over the cancan, a rowdy French vaudeville dance to which Offenbach gave a whole new career. It bubbled and bounced, and within a matter of months, it had become for Paris what the waltz was in Vienna—the throbbing heartbeat of a fun-mad city. "The idea of the cancan," said Mark Twain when he visited France, "is to dance as wildly, as noisily and as furiously as you can, to expose yourself as much as possible if you are a woman, and to kick as high as you can, no matter which sex you belong to. It is a whirl of shouts, laughter, furious music, a bewildering chaos of darting and interminable forms, stormy jerking and snatching of gay dresses, bobbing heads, flying arms, lightning-flashes of white-stockinged calves and dainty slippers in the air, and then a grand final rush, riot, terrific hubbub and wild stampede."[8]

The New World

And so Offenbach and his operettas continued to gain popularity, and by 1876 his fame had spread so far that he was invited to attend the one hundredth birthday party of the U.S.A. Offenbach didn't really want to go, but the Americans offered him so much money that he simply couldn't refuse. As soon as he boarded the ship he knew it was a mistake. The purser didn't stop telling him about his shipwreck on the last voyage; the ship's doctor got seasick and couldn't take care of the passengers; something went wrong with the propellers

[8] And you thought that Mark Twain sat home quietly in the evenings, writing about the Mississippi.

in the middle of the night; there was a terrible storm in the middle of the ocean. At last they reached New York, where a full tugboat load of musicians played them a welcome. Offenbach was wined and dined, and ten thousand people came to hear his first concert. Later, he gave several programs at the International Exposition in Philadelphia, and the crowds were even bigger. Usually Offenbach played only his own music, but one evening he also conducted a new piece by the twenty-two-year-old concertmaster of his orchestra. "Not bad," he told the young composer afterwards, "some day you ought to stop fooling around with marches and write an operetta." "I'll remember that," replied the concertmaster, whose name was John Philip Sousa.

Off-an'bach to Normal

When he wasn't wining or dining or conducting, Offenbach behaved just like any other tourist. He went to the theatres and to the opera and to the minstrel shows, and he took a Pullman to Niagara Falls, and he stared at the fire engines, and he rode the trolley cars in rush hour. Best of all, he girl-watched for hours at a time. "Out of a hundred American women," he said happily, "ninety are perfectly ravishing —going, coming, trotting, getting out of the way of street cars, lifting their dresses with the gesture of nature's coquette and discovering their exquisite ankles with an art all their own." Offenbach also decided that the women all carried purses so that "pickpockets would not have the indecent temptation to fumble in their pockets."[9]

Farewell

And so it was a converted German who sparked French

[9]Leave it to a Parisian to formulate a theory like that.

operetta and sent it breezing around the world, a fellow with long sideburns and velvet collars and patterned pants, sometimes unbuttoned. On his fifty-sixth birthday, a crowd of actors, singers and other musicians piled into fourteen buses after their various evening performances, and dropped in at midnight to serenade the composer with an impromptu concert of his own music. Offenbach was delighted, until he remembered that there was a sick old woman in the apartment below. Quickly he sent someone down to see if she was being disturbed. "Don't worry about me," she said. "I can't think of any way I'd rather die, than to the music of the cancan."

The March King as a Young Prince

Meanwhile, back on the bandstand, that young violinist who had been concertmaster in Offenbach's Philadelphia orchestra was still considering his advice and thinking about writing an operetta. In fact, one of John Philip Sousa's first big chances came when he was asked to compose the music for a road show called *The Phoenix*. The tour began in Streator, Illinois, and as soon as he got into town Sousa went to see the man from the musician's union to ask for five strings, four winds, a drum, and a two o'clock rehearsal. The representative looked up from his cement-mixing,[10] chomped on his cigar, and said, "Stranger, there are just two things that you don't want here. One is that you don't want any viola or celly and you don't want no flute, 'cause we ain't got 'em. The second thing you don't want is a rehearsal. We never have to rehearse here."

The Big Night

So, Sousa got up to conduct the overture without any

[10]Running a musician's union wasn't very profitable in those days.

rehearsal, and before he could turn a page, every man in the orchestra was playing in a different key. "It's in E-flat!" Sousa shouted, but the players just boomed louder so they wouldn't hear him. Each man screeched out his notes to the bitter end, and since some were slower than others, they finished one by one, like horses in a race. Sousa was boiling mad. He called the manager and the manager called the constable, and the constable threw the musicians out of the theatre. "I thought they didn't have to rehearse," John Philip complained. "They don't," explained the manager. "If they had a rehearsal, we'd have to throw them out *before* the performance."

The Coronation

Well, *The Phoenix* may have been a flop, but from its ashes rose a new American hero. John Philip Sousa decided to concentrate on something safer than road shows, and luckily he picked on marches. He wrote dozens and dozens of marches, and he dedicated them to everybody he could think of. He wrote one for the King of England and one for the Boy Scouts, and he wrote one for the Commissioner of Baseball and another for the Nobles of the Mystic Shrine, and eventually he even wrote a Golden Jubilee March for himself. Sousa would have preferred somebody else writing a march in his honor, but he had been conducting for fifty years already, and he couldn't wait forever.[11]

Side Line

Sousa also dedicated a march to a newspaper, and to

[11]Somebody had named the Sousaphone after him, but that wasn't the same thing. The Sousaphone is the tubbiest, funniest-looking instrument in the band, and John Philip was never even sure if he should be flattered or not.

everybody's astonishment, "The Washington Post" turned out to be the biggest dance fad of the Gay Nineties. The craze started when people discovered they could do a perfect two-step to the music, and soon they weren't dancing anything else. "Modern dances remind me of a pot of eels worming in and out," said John Philip, but the new step got more and more popular just the same. Soon it had pushed the waltz out of favor in America, and then it spread to Europe. They two-stepped to "Washington Post" on the Piazza di San Marco, and they two-stepped to it on the skating rinks of Paris. For a while, Sousa went around explaining to everybody that you were supposed to march to his music, not dance to it. Then he got the news that "Washington Post" had sold well over a million copies in sheet music alone. So he stopped explaining, and instead mentioned casually that you could do a nice two-step to "Semper Fidelis," too.

Secret Desires

In spite of all his successes, America's March King was still dreaming of writing operettas, and finally, before he got too old to dream, he wrote some. In fact, he wrote ten of them. They were simple, everyday stories of simple, everyday people, like *El Capitan,* a typical Sousa operetta, which takes place at the Gates of Tampoza,[12] where Scaramba plots with Don Errico Medigua to outwit Señor Amabile Pozzo. The first act finale is called "Bah Bah," which pretty well sums up the entire evening.

Audience Reaction

As it was, nobody seemed to care much for Sousa's operettas, but they sat through them to get to the marches. *El Capitan* is a good example. Sousa always put marches into his operettas after that one. Maybe he couldn't compose operettas too well, but he was no dope. Meanwhile, everybody was crazy about his marches, with or without operettas attached, and John Philip became one of the most famous men in the world. In London, the Regimental Bands struck up a Sousa tune for Queen Victoria's Diamond Jubilee celebrations, and in Germany, a Sousa march was played at the dedication of a statue of Wagner. Back home in Washington, D.C., Congress debated making "The Stars and Stripes Forever" our national

[12]When it's not taking place in the Plaza Limatamba.

anthem, and they probably would have done it, if anybody could have sung that darn piccolo part. And so, even though he didn't amount to much as an operetta composer, John Philip Sousa made millions happy with his music, and lived a long and contented life himself. "America doesn't want sadness," he said, "that's why I put sunshine into my music!" Come to think of it, I'm an anti-umbrella man myself.

MORE OPERETTAS:
Suppé and Strauss

Just about the time that Jacques Offenbach was introducing operettas to Paris, Franz von Suppé was making them popular in Vienna. Suppé wrote more than two hundred operettas, farces and other theatre pieces. Something must have gone wrong, because nobody produces them any more. All they do is play the overtures once or twice in a while.

Geography

Suppé had a very confusing start in life. His ancestry was spotty,[1] and even though his Italian parents were of Belgian descent, he spent most of his life in Austria. Eventually he became known as "the German Offenbach," but that didn't make things any clearer. After all, Offenbach really *was* born in Germany, while Suppé only dropped in to visit every so often. Anyway, his parents couldn't make up their minds what to name him, and since both refused to give up their pet choices, they had the boy christened Francesco Ezechiale Ermenegildo Cavaliere Suppé Demelli. Naturally, Suppé couldn't wait to change his name, and as soon as he moved to Vienna, he did it. He added a "von."

Bibliography

The main reason nobody produces any of Suppé's oper-

---

[1] No joke, he was a Dalmatian.

ettas any more is that his plots were even more awful than those of the other operas this book is all about. The closest he ever came to a decent story was when he made an operetta out of the Pygmalion legend and called it *My Fair Galatea*. The rest of the time he wasted his energy on things like *Fatinitza,* which is about a general named Count Timofay Gabrilovitsch Kantschakoff who falls in love with a lieutenant named Michailoff,[2] and *Die Kartenschlägerin,* which is about ... well, don't ask. Suppé kept running out of ideas, too. He composed one operetta where every single tune was lifted from something by Schubert, and then, when Wagner wasn't looking, he put out two others called *Lohengeld* and *Tannenhäuser.* (Once when he was really stuck, Suppé sat down and wrote a cookbook.) Still another of his operettas tells about a fellow who makes love to a peasant girl while his wife (disguised as a statue) tries to get the goods on him. With stories like that, it's what's up front that counts, so it's fortunate that Suppé did come through with some pretty nifty overtures.

Praeludium

Speaking of overtures, I've always had the feeling that a lot of them are much too good to be wasted on operas and operettas. In the opera house, the main function of the overture is to provide incidental music for coat-fixing, program-rustling, neighbor-greeting, and binocular-looking-to-see-who-else-is-there. Overtures are sometimes used for throat-clearing accompaniments too, although most veteran opera-goers prefer to wait for the love scenes, when the acoustics are better. I can think of other advantages of listening to overtures without the operas tacked on afterwards. They're shorter, and they have all the best tunes.

2!

Waltzes

At this time the waltz craze was sweeping Europe, and another of Suppé's accomplishments was to lend it a broom. In the mid-1800's, you know, the waltz was considered highly scandalous in some quarters,[3] and Suppé made it seem a touch more respectable by setting polite words to it. It didn't matter to some people, though. The waltz was the first dance where the partners actually held each other close, and the moralists were shocked at the abominable sight of "a lady permitting a man to encircle her with his arms and to press the contour of her waist." Every night the moralists would flock down to the dance halls to watch the contours and get shocked all over again. Soon, reformed Dancing Masters were publishing big exposés, revealing the ballrooms to be "hotbeds of vice within whose treacherous embrace so many sweet young souls have been whirled to perdition."

Vienna

With recommendations like that, it was only a matter of time before the waltz became the most popular dance on the Continent, and nowhere did it catch on with greater glitter than in the city of Vienna. Nobody cared that the skittle alleys had been scuttled, or that theatres weren't putting on wolf-fights any more.[4] The simple fact is that everybody was too busy waltzing to bother about anything else. The dances used to last from ten at night until seven the next morning, and couples would have contests to see who could waltz more times in succession from one end of the hall to the other. It got to the

[3]About three quarters, to be exact.

[4]Some theatres had specialized in bear-fights, but they were also closed down. Even the lion-eating-lamb exhibitions were going out of business.

point where some ballrooms had special chambers where expectant mothers could give birth after indulging in one last dance.[5] From the Emperor down to the lowliest shopgirl, everyone in Vienna was hopelessly waltz-crazy. And so, it was only natural that the city should give birth to the greatest waltz composer of them all.

The Strauss Family

Johann Strauss was the incomparable Waltz King of Vienna. So was his father. In fact, Strauss's father was also named Johann, which sometimes made it a little tricky to tell which King had the crown. Johann Jr. had a couple of brothers who wrote waltzes also, but they weren't in the same league. Eduard studied to be a diplomat, and Josef invented a street-sweeping machine, and both of them only entered the waltz business to help their brother when he got too busy.

King I

Papa Strauss was born in the Flossgasse, which didn't bother him at all. His father was an alehouse keeper, and even as a little boy Johann Sr. used to pour beer into the body of his violin to make the tone more mellow. When he grew up, he got smart and started pouring the beer directly into his own body. This didn't help the fiddle tone, but Johann felt mellow as anything. Sometimes he got so mellow that he couldn't think of any new waltzes. When that happened, he simply took other people's tunes and turned *them* into waltzes. He did it to an aria from Mozart's *The Magic Flute,* and to a theme from Beethoven's "Kreutzer" Sonata, and to "God Save the Queen." To that one, even Queen Victoria danced. She probably thought it was the least she could do.

[5]Other ballrooms had special chambers where indulgent young ladies could become expectant mothers.

Like Father, Like Son, Only More So

Everything was going well with Johann Sr. until Johann Jr. came along. The kid was only six years old when he began composing little waltzes, and right away his father started getting nervous. Papa Strauss was the musical toast of Vienna, and he didn't want to get burned. He also knew a rival when he heard one, and for years he did everything he could think of to discourage his son's interest in music. He alternately wheedled and threatened, and he told little Johann horrible stories about the struggles musicians had to go through to make ends meet. He was wasting his time, of course. Johann Jr. didn't give a schnitzel about meeting ends, and he kept on getting more musical all the time. Pretty soon, Schani, as the boy was nicknamed, was secretly taking violin lessons from his father's concertmaster. When he found out about it, Papa Strauss was so outraged that he locked the fiddle away in a cupboard and made Schani take a job as a bank clerk. Luckily, Mama Strauss had an extra key to the cupboard, so Schani got his fiddle back the very next day, and started practicing even harder.[6]

Pass the Crown, Please

Finally, in October of 1844, when he was only nineteen, Schani hired an orchestra and let all Vienna know that he, too, was going into the music business. Papa Strauss was outraging more than ever. First he tried to stop the concert, and when he couldn't, he sent a whole crowd of friends over to boo and hiss and to turn the debut into as big a fiasco as possible. Everybody in town knew of the rivalry, and so many of them

[6]Mama Strauss might not have gone against her husband had she not been fairly annoyed with him right about then. Johann Sr. had set up a second household with Emilie Trampusch in the Kumpgasse on the other side of the Schwedenbrücke. That's enough to annoy anybody.

squeezed into the dance hall that night that there was no room to dance. It didn't matter. Schani stepped out onto the stage, flashed a broad smile, and began to play, conducting the orchestra at the same time with his fiddle bow. Papa Strauss's stooges made their rude noises on schedule, but to their amazement they were immediately shushed by the enthusiastic audience, which went on to greet the young man's musical magic with cheers and tears of joy. They made Schani encore almost every piece, and they applauded so much that he had to repeat the closing waltz nineteen times.[7]

Bonus

At last, just when everybody was collapsing with exhaustion, Schani waved his hands for silence, quietly turned to his orchestra, and began "Lorelei Rhine Echoes," his *father's* most famous waltz. That did it. The place went wild, and the sentimental Viennese, including the men who had originally come to sabotage the performance, rushed forward and swept Schani away on their shoulders, carrying him in triumph around the hall and then out into the street. Johann could have named two or three more comfortable ways to travel, but he was too happy to complain. After all, his most glowing dreams had come true, not to mention his father's most horrible nightmares. As one reporter wrote, after that unforgettable concert, "Good evening, Father Strauss. Good morning, Son Strauss."

Career Man

And so the son rose, and by mid-afternoon, Schani had an

[7]Which reminds me of the story of the second-rate tenor at La Scala who was so happily surprised when somebody yelled "Encore!" after his big aria, that he promptly sang the whole thing again. More shouts of "Encore" went up, and the delighted tenor went through it twice more. Finally, the same voice roared out from the balcony: "Again! Do it again! And keep doing it until you get it right!"

organization of several hundred people going full tilt—singers, copyists, orchestra men, assistant conductors, even press agents. Sometimes he had three orchestras playing simultaneously in different ballrooms in Vienna, with the Maestro himself only stopping by for a brief personal appearance in each. And all the while, he composed hundreds of waltzes. When Strauss wasn't composing waltzes, he was composing mazurkas (a mazurka is a little like a waltz, if you have hiccups), and when he wasn't composing mazurkas, he was composing polonaises, gavottes, polkas and galops (a galop is a little like a polka, if you're a horse).[8]

Down by the Riverside

Oddly enough, Strauss's most glorious waltz, "The Beautiful Blue Danube," was a total flop at first. Maybe it's because everybody in Vienna knew that the Danube isn't blue at all. It's gray sometimes, and dirty green other times. It's also sludgy, reedy, murky and smelly. But blue, no. Another trouble was that Strauss wrote the waltz for the Men's Choral Society of Vienna, which meant that it had to have words. The words were written by Josef Weyl, a local poet who could write beautiful verses the way the Danube was blue. I just happen to have some of them with me, now that you ask:

> Vienna, be gay!
> And what for, pray?
> A glimmer of light
> To us is night.
> Carnival's come?
> Ho-ho, ha-hum.[9]

The singers almost went on strike when they were given

[8]Strauss's most famous polka is "Tritsch-Tratsch," while his best galop is called "Klipp-Klapp." See?

[9]I have more, but it's downhill from there on.

stuff like that, and the worst of it was that they were so busy hating the lyrics that they missed liking the music. The piece was dropped after only two performances. "I don't mind about the waltz so much," complained Strauss to his brother Josef, "it's just that the thing has such a nice, elaborate ending."

Second Chance

Schani needn't have worried. You can't keep a good river down, and within a year or two "The Blue Danube" came bubbling back as cheerful as ever. Its popularity spread to Berlin, then to Paris, then around the rest of Europe, and finally across the seas to America, where it resulted in the most fantastic performance of all. It happened during the Boston Peace Jubilee of 1872, a little party masterminded by the famous showman, Pat Gilmore. Gilmore had built an intimate concert hall for the occasion, holding a mere hundred thousand people, and he hired an orchestra of eleven hundred players, plus a couple of dozen brass bands, in case anything went wrong with the orchestra. He also brought in a chorus of several thousand voices, a hundred anvils, with red-shirted firemen to bang them, and a bass drum some eighteen feet in diameter. Then he lined up a whole row of cannons, electrically wired for consecutive firing on the first beat of each measure.[10]

Guest Appearance

What gave the Jubilee its crowning touch was the in-person appearance of the Waltz King himself. Strauss hated

[10]When Gilmore said he was going to shoot the works, he wasn't kidding.

the idea of the long ocean voyage to America, but he was persuaded to come over by an enormous fee of $100,000, plus free transportation for him, his wife, his two servants, and his huge Newfoundland dog. On the day of the concert the bewildered composer climbed nervously up a specially constructed lookout tower, clutching a long, illuminated baton. Before him stretched the monstrous performing forces on the field of battle, with one hundred assistant conductors, each armed with binoculars, stationed at strategic points across the vast acreage to help guide the musical traffic. Poor Strauss was too shaken to comment then and there, but when he had safely escaped back to Vienna, he said plenty. "A cannon shot rang out," he recalled, in one of his more printable statements, "a gentle hint for the twenty thousand to begin playing 'The Blue Danube.' I gave the signal, my hundred assistant conductors followed me as quickly as they could, and then there broke out an unholy row such as I shall never forget. . . ."

Hair Today

The only really happy participant in the whole affair was one of the two servants. It seems that a fad had developed during Strauss's visit, and Bostonians were falling all over themselves in their anxiety to get a lock of the composer's hair as a souvenir. The servant let it be known that he could supply the demand in return for a slight consideration, and he did a land-office business shipping out bags full of the stuff to delighted customers. It wasn't Strauss's hair at all, obviously, merely locks deftly clipped from the abundant coat of his Newfoundland. How about that for a shaggy dog story? And a true one, too.

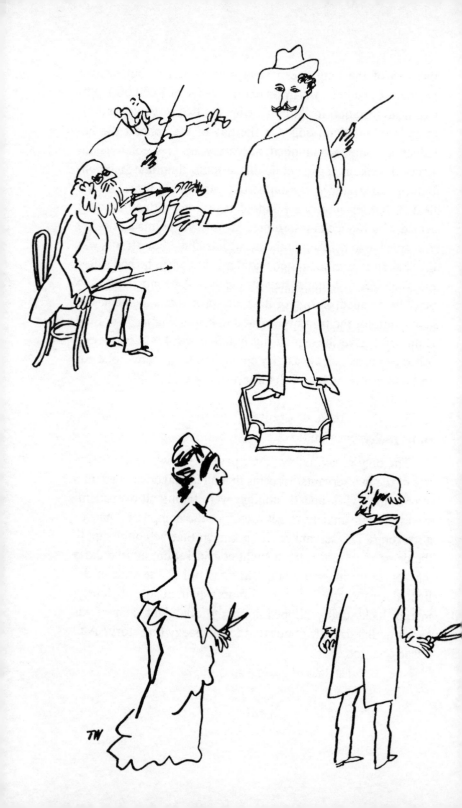

Stage Call

For many years, Johann was doing so handsomely with his waltzes that he never gave operettas a second thought. Possibly he wouldn't have given them a first thought either, if Jacques Offenbach had not come to Vienna to conduct. "Some day," said Offenbach when he was introduced to Strauss, "you ought to stop fooling around with waltzes and write an operetta." Strauss just laughed and went back to his waltzes, but he reckoned without his wife, Jetty. Jetty had been an operetta singer in her younger days, and she didn't forget easily.[11] She remembered very distinctly how much money Offenbach's operettas were making, and she started pestering Johann to write some operettas, too. Strauss was an accommodating fellow, so he tried and tried, but somehow everything came out sounding like waltzes.

Trickery

Eventually, there was only one thing left to do. Jetty tiptoed into Johann's studio one night, secretly took a big pile of unpublished compositions from his desk, and carted them over to the opera house. The manager, who was in on the deal, summoned a hack librettist to put lyrics to the tunes and string together a makeshift plot around them. The first Strauss knew about it was when a couple of singers dropped by to compliment him on the nice arias. In a panic, he rushed over to the opera house, and there was the whole show already in rehearsal. It was perfectly dreadful, and what's more, the manager insisted that he would go on with it unless somebody came through with a substitute. Strauss was stuck. He realized that he had to deliver a decent operetta no matter what.

[11]She forgot to tell Johann about her illegitimate son, but that was accidental.

[183]

Operetta Fever

Once he'd begun, he discovered that writing operettas wasn't nearly so difficult as he had thought. Everything still came out sounding like waltzes, but now Strauss pretended not to notice, and the songs just tumbled from his pen. His first operetta was called *The Merry Wives of Vienna,* and Johann had so much fun composing it that he didn't even get angry when the manager decided not to produce it after all.[12] Strauss's second operetta was called *Indigo and the Forty Thieves,* and each thief must have demanded his own aria, since the show ran four hours.[13] Even so, it was a big hit, and after that, there was no stopping him. Strauss composed one operetta after another, and even when all the good plots were used up, he kept turning them out just the same. Towards the end, he was so desperate for stories that he wrote operettas like *Blind Man's Bluff* and *Simplizius Simplicissimus* and even *The Queen's Spitzentuch.*[14] After a while, Johann got interested in grand opera too, and it was he who conducted the Vienna première of the Prelude to Wagner's *Tristan and Isolde.* Later, at Bayreuth, Wagner reciprocated by conducting Strauss's waltz, "Wine, Women and Song."

Bats and Balls

Strauss's most famous operetta came long before he got desperate, although you could never tell it from the plot.

[12]Remind me to tell you about the merry wives of Strauss, some day. Especially #2, who got so annoyed at him for marrying #3 that she walked up and down in front of his house with a picket sign.

[13]The two big numbers were "Geschmiedet fest an starrer Felswand" and "Ja, so singt man in der Stadt, wo ich geboren," which slowed things down fast.

[14]Sometimes, I think Strauss was pretty lucky everything came out sounding like waltzes.

That's the one called *Die Fledermaus* (which means "The Bat") when it's not being called *The Merry Countess, A Masked Ball,* or *Fly by Night*. Strauss wasn't the least bothered by the plot. The minute he saw the libretto,[15] he knew the operetta was going to be the best thing he ever wrote. For one thing, the story was so ridiculous that everybody was bound to give their full attention to the music. Besides, the whole second act took place at a lavish ball, which meant that he could stick in as many waltzes as he wanted to, without apologizing.

Genius at Work

Pretty soon, Strauss got so excited about the project that he sent away all the servants, locked himself up in his country house, and for the next forty-three days paid absolutely no attention to anything else except the composition of *Die Fledermaus*. Sometimes he would neglect to eat breakfast until three in the afternoon; often he would get up in the middle of the night, jot down a tune on the cuff of his nightshirt, and then work it into a song until way past daybreak.

Original Cast

The setting of *Die Fledermaus* is "a watering place near a large town," but since nobody gets to see either the town or water, you might as well forget about that part of it. The main characters are Gabriel von Eisenstein, when he isn't pretending to be the Marquis Renard; Rosalinde, his wife, when she isn't pretending to be a Hungarian Countess; Adele, her chambermaid, when she isn't pretending to be Olga the Actress; Frank, the jailor, when he isn't pretending to be the Chevalier Chagrin; and Alfred, the singing teacher, when he

[15]The libretto was stolen by Genee and Haffner from a play by Meilhac and Halèvy who swiped it from something by Roderich Benedix. I don't know where Benedix got it.

isn't pretending to be Gabriel von Eisenstein. The only person who isn't pretending to be anybody else is Prince Orlovsky, and he's always played by a woman.

Story Line

As the curtain goes up, we see an empty room in the Eisenstein house. This is a crucial moment in the operetta, because it's the last time anybody knows for sure what's going on. After that, the plot is one mass of confusion, with mistaken identities, people making love to their own wives, and other absurdities. In many productions of *Die Fledermaus*, performers wander in from other operas and sing music by other composers,[16] and by the time the chorus gets to the big number at the end of Act Two, the singers are so befuddled that they gurgle things like "hu hu hu hu" and "dui-du, dui-du, la la la, la la la."[17] In fact, the premise of the operetta seems to be that if you've had enough champagne, you won't notice all the holes in the plot. Well, darn the holes in the plot! Strauss wrote some of his most marvelous music for *Die Fledermaus*, including a laughing song, a drinking song, and a Hungarian Czardas (which is something like a polka if you limp a little), and that's what counts.[18]

Finale

And so, Johann Strauss continued writing beautiful music, and all over the world people continued to sing it and dance

[16]There's a recording out which actually has a duet from *Annie Get Your Gun* stuck right in the middle of the party scene.

[17]You don't believe me? Look it up right there in the libretto.

[18]If you look up Czardas in the Harvard Brief Dictionary of Music, you'll find it defined as "incorrect spelling for Csardas." I've seen snooty dictionaries in my day, but really!

to it, as I guess they always will. Gustav Mahler produced *Die Fledermaus* on the stage of the Austrian Court Opera, Anton Rubinstein played Strauss waltzes at his piano recitals, Hans von Bülow scheduled them alongside the Beethoven symphonies, and yet another composer responded to an autograph request by scribbling down a few notes of "The Blue Danube." Underneath the music, he wrote: "Unfortunately, not by Johannes Brahms." As for Strauss himself, he grew old gracefully and happily, working until the last, and especially proud that his waltzes had become the symbol of his birthplace. "If it be true that I have some talent," he said, when notables from every corner of the world gathered to pay their respects on the fiftieth anniversary of his debut, "I owe its development to my beloved city. Vienna! I drink to her! May she grow and prosper!"

Underture

All good things must end, eventually, and I'm afraid our book just has. It's a pity too, because I was just getting warmed up. I was going to tell you about Tony Vivaldi and his all-girl Orchestra, and Paganini, who had to publish a letter from his mother to prove to people that he wasn't the Devil's son, and Brahms, whose pants fell down in the middle of a concert.

As a matter of fact, I could write a book about all the things I didn't get to put in this one, and some day soon, maybe I will.

So let's not call this an ending. Let's just pause for a while, until we meet again. Hopefully, it will be one of your favorite intermissions also.

Curtain Down